America's Forgotten Heritage

A Collection of Resources for
Youth and Families on
America's Christian History

Carol B. Olsen

America's
Forgotten Heritage

© 2011 Carol B. Olsen, Parent Educator
ISBN 978-0-615-41203-0

All rights reserved. Printed in the USA.

Illustration: Mollie Sieve Olsen
Art Educator and Illustrator

Editor: Joan Sherman
Marketing Communications, LLC

Graphic Design: Barbara With

All Scriptural quotes taken from
New International Version (NIV)

Riding the Truth Press
www.AmericasForgottenHeritage.com
Americasheritage@gmail.com

Dedication

To our forefathers
… all the men and women who pledged their lives, their fortunes, and their sacred honor for the protection of the Christian principles upon which this country was founded.

To a friend
… who was surprised to hear that our country had a firm foundation on Christian principles and was unsettled about how contrary the teaching she received in her many years of schooling and advanced study was to this truth. She showed me the need and strengthened my resolve to continue sharing the truth of the founding era and the Christian foundation of our country.

To our grandchildren
… in the great hope that they may understand, appreciate, and work to honor and preserve the Christian foundation of our country.

With grateful appreciation to:
- My Lord, who answered my prayers.
- My husband, Neil, my biggest supporter.
- My sister, Janet Averill, who opened my eyes.
- Becky Danielson, the encourager of all encouragers.
- Sue Payne, a visionary in children's ministry.
- Michael Chapman, a source of abundant information.

Carol B. Olsen

A Recommendation from Michael J. Chapman

"Rare and Refreshing"

For more than 20 years, I have studied the original writings and manuscripts of America's Founding Fathers, and I have come to the conclusion that the only way to solve America's many problems is to seek their wisdom.

Did you know that our Founders—the 220 or so men who signed the Declaration of Independence, the Constitution, and the Bill of Rights—wrote more than 80,000 volumes that cover every issue under the sun? Why is it that you cannot find but a handful of them in reprint at America's public libraries?

I think it's because they based their ideas for government on Christian principles—and Christianity is no longer held in high regard among those who dominate the institutions of government, media and academia. Few then, bother to dig down to the root – to seek the wisdom of Washington, Jefferson, Adams, Franklin, Ames, or other forgotten founders for answers to contemporary social problems.

That is why it's so rare and refreshing to find a book that carefully chronicles the path to success that our Founders set this great nation upon. There have been a few: Barton, Eidsmoe, Foster, Millard, and DeMar come to mind. But now, add Carol Olsen to the list. Not so much because her material is completely new, but because she brings the Founders' knowledge to a concise form at a readership level that can captivate and teach America's youth – our future citizens, voters and leaders. America's Forgotten Heritage is a book of knowledge that will help our youth understand the forgotten ideas that can, again, provide America's answers – even before they can fully grasp the questions.

Carol Olsen magnificently captures the vital information that I believe every adult needs to know to become a fully informed citizen. She interjects conversations with her own children and lessons that can be a guide toward sharing insights with yours. Olsen's book may even create that spark to set your children on the path toward becoming the future answer to America's next, greatest challenge. America's Forgotten Heritage is must reading for anyone who wants to understand the Christian ideas that made America successful in the first place, and remind you what it will take to bring us back from the brink of disaster.

Michael J. Chapman
American History Researcher
www.americanheritageresearch.com
Author of *Dreamers of a Godless Utopia*

The General Principle of Christianity
upon which the United States was forged:

"The general principles on which the Fathers achieved independence were the only principles in which that beautiful assembly of young gentlemen could unite ... And what were the general principles? I answer, the general principle of Christianity, in which all were united."

John Adams
In a letter written to Thomas Jefferson, June 28, 1813

Table of Contents

Foreword 9
How Well Do You Know Your American Christian History? . 14
Introduction: Why Teach Our Christian Heritage? 15
Level Setting: What's a Worldview? 19

Part I: Stepping Back in Time: Personal Stories
1613: Pocahontas - A Christian Sister 31
1620: Olivia's Story of the Mayflower 33
1621: Squanto - A Christian Brother 41
1621: William Bradford - The Beginning of
      American Free Enterprise 43

Part II: Learn from Family Stories & Conversations
God's Hand on the Newcomers 47
A Nation of Prayer 55
Our Constitutional Republic 63

Part III: Spotlight: Influential Founding Fathers
George Washington: The Preacher of Providence 71
Jonathan Edwards & George Whitefield:
      The Great Awakening 79
Noah Webster: "Education without the Bible is useless" ... 81
Signers of the Constitution: All Men are Created Equal..... 83

Part IV: Foundational Symbols & Documents
1620: The Mayflower Compact 89
1751: The Liberty Bell 91
1776: The Declaration of Independence 93
1787: The United States Constitution 99
1787: The Preamble of the United States Constitution .. 105
Separation From Church and State
    Is This in the Constitution?.................... 107

Part V: Just for Fun
The Dollar Bill 111
The Dollar Bill Quiz 114
The Liberty Bell Quiz 115
Did You Know? Facts About Our Christian Heritage 116

Appendix
Summary of Memory Verses 119
Bibliography 120
Additional Resources.............................. 122
Meet the Author: Carol B. Olsen 123

Permission is granted to use any of this information for not-for-profit educational programs, provided references are cited. All other uses, please contact the author.

Foreword

This timely book provides a resource on "America's Forgotten Heritage" for young and old alike. Its storybook style and use of original documents illustrates how the Founding Fathers applied Biblical discernment to the development of our nation's founding documents.

My wife, Carol, has a passion for this critical topic from a historical perspective, but also because the Bible and the Christian faith was central in the lives of the Founders and their families. She has taught America's Christian heritage for several years in churches and small home groups. Carol and her sister, Janet, are serious advocates and promoters of our Christian heritage and have reached out to many. You might say it's a family tradition.

As you read this book, please realize and appreciate the overarching Biblical views that guided and directed the early colonists – our Founding Fathers. God has had a providential hand in all beginnings, and we see this very clearly in the founding era of our country (1620-1789).

God settled this continent over a period of time using a variety of people groups. He started with the various Indian tribes and nations followed by the Europeans, i.e., Pilgrims, Puritans, Quakers, adventurers, developers, etc. **"Then God blessed Noah and his sons, saying to them, 'Be fruitful and increase in number and fill the earth.'"** Genesis 9:1. When it was time to organize the country as a free and independent nation, He chose God-fearing men and women to lead the way.

The establishing of the nation into a Constitutional Republic was one of the largest collective acts of Biblical discernment ever applied and documented. How do we know this? The availability of original documents is overwhelming. These include newspapers, sermons, letters, notes from the

Constitutional and Continental Conventions, congressional records, and the Federalist Papers just to name a few. It was a time when formal written communication was the standard, and it was preserved.

Education

Almost every child in early America was educated. This was largely due to the colonists' desire for their children to be able to read the Scriptures. Parents saw it as their responsibility, and not that of government, to provide education. They understood the Biblical command of Deuteronomy 6:6-7 **"And these words, which I am commanding you today, shall be on your heart; and you shall teach them diligently to your sons..."** and Ephesians 6:4 **"Fathers, do not provoke your children to anger; but bring them up in the discipline and instruction of the Lord."**

In the colonial years, America's education was primarily centered in the home. Home education was sometimes supplemented by tutors or schools, but even here the responsibility and the bulk of the child's education rested in the home.

"...This was solely the case until a child was the age of eight or nine. At that point, some children had tutors to further instruct them; an even smaller number attended a school ... ministers were generally the tutors. If there were too many children in the minister's community for him to go to each home to tutor, he would receive a group of children into his home. These were the first grammar schools and began in the late 1600's."[1]

Samuel L. Blumenfeld says, "Of the 117 men who signed the Declaration of Independence, the Articles of Confederation and the Constitution, only one in four had gone to college. They were educated by parents, church schools, tutors, academies, apprenticeship, and by themselves."[2]

Biblical examples from God's Word

Let's look at three examples from God's word to see how Biblical principles shaped our country.

1. Moses – Establish local and national civil authorities which are the foundations of the republic form of government

Moses had a serious problem leading his new nation, but he received divine guidance from his father-in-law, Jethro. **"But select capable men from all the people-- men who fear God, trustworthy men who hate dishonest gain-- and appoint them as officials over thousands, hundreds, fifties and tens. Have them serve as judges for the people at all times, but have them bring every difficult case to you; the simple cases they can decide themselves. That will make your load lighter, because they will share it with you. If you do this and God so commands, you will be able to stand the strain, and all these people will go home satisfied."** Exodus 18:21-23. Here we have the establishment of the division of our civil authorities from the national to the local...."v.21 (partial), **"appoint them as officials over thousands, hundreds, fifties and tens."**

2. Paul – Hold fast to Biblical truth in spite of the culture

The apostle Paul was very concerned because the church had come under attack by the false teaching of the culture. He writes, **"See to it that no one takes you captive through hollow and deceptive philosophy, which depends on human tradition and the basic principles of this world rather than on Christ."** Colossians 2:8 The Founding Fathers rejected both the false teaching of the European "enlightenment" and the monarchy rule. These were a direct threat to their Biblical worldview. Outside influences were rejected during this period. One must recognize that statements in the Declaration of Independence such as, "We hold these truths to be self-evident, that all men are created equal, they are **endowed by their Creator** with certain inalienable rights….." (emphasis added), would not have been declared from within a man-centered philosophy. Only a Christ-centered view could cause the Founding Fathers to write this document with this language.

3. Paul – Use Scripture to evaluate and rightly discern

The apostle Paul was also very concerned with how the church would evaluate and discern rightly from within worldly influences."**Test everything. Hold on to the good. Avoid every kind of evil."** 1 Thessalonians 5:21-22. This type of exhortation by Paul to the church at Thessalonica corresponds directly to the Founders' actions. They sorted and filtered from Scripture and the writings from men such as Locke, Blackstone, Montesquieu, Wycliffe, and others to find the Biblical guidance and authority that solidified their understanding.

Home grown and Biblically sown

As we look back at our founding documents, we can reflect on them admirably -- or critically. This book allows you to look at them for what they are … written by men who used Scripture as their guide. Were they perfect? No. Did these men have wisdom beyond their education? Yes. Where did it come from? It came from the Holy Spirit and generations of home schooling that allowed them to understand and apply the moral standards of the Bible to their times. They also understood from the pulpit, **"The fear of the LORD is the beginning of wisdom; all who follow his precepts have good understanding. To him belongs eternal praise."** Psalm 111:10. These founding documents were home grown and Biblically sown.

In the context of this founding era, let's use this verse to remember and honor the actions of these brave men and their families:

> **"If you hold to my teaching, you are really my disciples. Then you will know the truth, and the truth will set you free."** John 8:31-32

With love for Jesus Christ, family, and country,
Neil Olsen

---

[1] Mark Beliles & Stephen McDowell, *America's Providential History*, p 102-103

[2] Mark Beliles & Stephen McDowell, *America's Providential History*, p 105

How Well Do You Know Your American Christian History?

Take this quick quiz and find out! (Answers can be found on the page indicated.)

- What phrase is written on the Liberty Bell? (Page 91)
- According to the Mayflower Compact, what were the reasons why the Pilgrims came to the New World? (Page 90)
- Who is called the father of the U.S. Constitution? (Page 99)
- Who was the most famous Native American baptized a Christian in 1613? (Page 32)
- What was the name of the first textbook published in America? (Page 81)
- The Founding Fathers often mentioned "the providence of God." What does that mean? (Page 73)
- What book was most often quoted in the Founding Father's personal and public writings? (Page 17)
- When the Constitution Convention was at a complete stalemate over how to determine representation, what did Benjamin Franklin request? (Page 60)

Introduction: Why Teach Our Christian Heritage?

Memory Verses
- Psalms 33:12 – **"Blessed is the nation whose God is the LORD, the people He chose for His inheritance."**
- Hosea 4:6 – **"My people are destroyed from lack of knowledge ..."**

    The United States of America had a glorious Christian beginning, and our children have the right to learn and celebrate this fact. I have compiled this booklet in the hopes that youth everywhere will learn to appreciate our American Christian heritage.

    Today our children learn little concerning the Judeo-Christian principles that were so prominent and fundamental to the founding of the United States. Public schools and most teachers are convinced that they need not, nor can they legally, teach the overriding Christian influence of our heritage. This part of history has been quietly and systematically deleted from textbooks and curriculum. Our American Christian heritage is all but forgotten. Even our National Parks that teach heritage have conveniently and unfortunately left the faith of our Founders and the influence of the Bible out of public domain.

    Are we a Christian nation? Today that is debatable, but the fact that we were founded on Christian principles is not. One of the very first governmental documents written in America was the Mayflower Compact, which set up a system to work for the common good. It clearly states the purpose of the endeavor was **"... for the glory of God and the advancement of the Christian faith."**[1]

Our Founding Fathers wanted the freedom to be able to live their lives according to the Scriptures. All the colonial charters written during the founding era had the same purpose. Men like George Washington, John Adams, John Quincy Adams, George Mason, and Fischer Aims all relied on the providence of God to direct and protect the beginnings of our new nation. They believed that **rights come from God,** not man or government, and could not be taken away. Historical written documents, letters, and the congressional records are all positive proof of their reliance upon God.

> This new government was based on the idea that unalienable rights come from God, not government or a dictator, and that civil rulers or legislators obtain their authority only through the consent of the governed by election.

In 1831, a noted French author, statesman and social philosopher, Alexis deTocqueville, came to the United States to determine what it was that made America great. He traveled from coast to coast and talked to many. He came to the following conclusion: "Not until I went into the churches of America and heard her pulpits aflame with righteousness did I understand the secret of her genius and power... **The Americans combine the notions of Christianity and of liberty so intimately in their minds that it is impossible to make them conceive of one without the other."** [2]

The Mayflower Compact was not the only historical document that included Christian ideals. The United States Constitution was written by ordinary men from different walks of life, but these Founding Fathers all shared a Biblical worldview and applied it to the new and innovative form of government.

Where did the Founding Fathers get their new (and seemingly radical) ideas? What sources did they use in their writings, speeches and written documents? The University of Houston conducted a research project to determine what truly influenced our Founding Fathers. They assembled 15,000 writings of the founding era over a period of 10 years and were able to isolate and source some 3,154 direct quotes. The quotes came from the following:

- 8.3% - Baron Charles de Montesquieu, a Christian philosopher
- 7.9% - William Blackstone, a British Christian barrister and author of *Commentaries of Law*, a work based on Biblical principles
- 2.9% - John Locke, a British Christian philosopher and political scientist
- 34% - The Bible[3]

These Founding Fathers had what Dr. Frances Schaefer, an influential 20th century Christian philosopher, called a "Christian consensus."[4] They shared a Christian (or Biblical) worldview and applied it to the new (and completely unheard of to this point) form of government. 52 of the 55 representatives who were part of the Constitutional Convention were openly verbal about their faith in Jesus Christ and were members of an orthodox Christian church.[5] They understood the sinful nature of man and man's self-serving ways. To prevent future tyranny by the government (man), they incorporated the separation of powers (executive, legislative, and judicial) and the dividing of authority into workable levels (local, state, federal). The basis for these ideas can be found in the Bible, which also provides for the basis of law. This is why the 10 commandments are chiseled into the wall of the United States Supreme Court.

These early Americans wanted everyone to be educated so they could read the Bible and know God's will. They thought this would prevent the abuse of Christianity and the name of Jesus Christ, which had been done in abhorrent campaigns, such as the Crusades and the Inquisition. Unfortunately, knowing scripture did not stop their acceptance of the world's evil practice of slavery, and that will forever be a blot on American history. However, many Founding Fathers fought against slavery, purposely kept the right to own slaves out of the Constitution and fervently prayed that slavery would self destruct. Many founded abolitionist societies. [6]

No one should be afraid of history and no one should be ignorant of the beliefs of our Founding Fathers. Hosea 4:6 gives us a powerful message:"**... my people are destroyed by lack of knowledge.**"

I hope this booklet will help prepare you -- and future generations -- to meet the challenges in what feels like an increasingly anti-Christian culture. It has been prepared with love for our Lord and Savior - Jesus Christ and our country.

Carol B. Olsen

[1] Mayflower Compact
[2] Chalfant, John W. *America - A Call to Greatness,* p11
[3] Barton, David. *America's Godly Heritage*, p 9
[4] LaHaye, Tim. *Faith of Our Founding Fathers.* p 33
[5] LaHaye, Tim. *Faith of Our Founding Fathers.* p 3
[6] Chalfant, John W. *America - A Call to Greatness*, p 48

Level Setting: What's a Worldview?

Memory Verses
- 1 Thessalonians 5:21-22 – *"Test everything. Hold on to the good. Avoid every kind of evil."*
- Colossians 2:8 – *"See to it that no one takes you captive through hollow and deceptive philosophy, which depends on human tradition and the basic principles of this world rather than on Christ."*
- John 8:31b-32 – *"Jesus said, 'If you hold to my teaching, you are really my disciples. Then you will know the truth, and the truth will set you free.'"*

Lilly and her new friend, Krissy, hurried home from school, talking about their American history class.

"I wonder why Mrs. Webber didn't mention anything about the importance of the Christian religion in the founding of our country. It isn't even in our history book, but I know it is true because my grandfather talks about it a lot," Lilly said, as she walked faster to keep up with Krissy.

Krissy said, "That's easy. It just isn't important. If Miss Webber didn't mention it and our book leaves it out, it means it wasn't important. You remember, she talked about those philosophers from Europe, you know ... "the Enlightenment." They are the ones who influenced the writing of our Constitution and everything else. Anyway, how would God play a role in anything?"

"Don't you believe in God?" asked Lilly, a little uncertain.

"No. My parents say that God probably does not exist, because if He did we wouldn't have all these problems of war and hunger. You know, all that stuff," said Krissy.

With that, Krissy ran toward her house saying, "Lilly, I have to go, but I'll call you when I get home. I need to check something out."

Shortly after Lilly arrived home and pulled out her favorite snack of sea salt chips, her cell phone rang. Lilly answered and was pleased to hear Krissy's voice.

The Invitation ... and the Problem

"Lilly, can you go to the movie theater with me on Saturday? I want to see that new "R" rated movie. I have seen some before and they are really cool and fun to watch."

Hesitantly, Lilly said, "We can't see that kind of movie; we're not old enough."

"Oh, don't worry about that. I know how to get in, trust me. I've done it before and it is so cool -- and you can't believe what they show on the screen," Krissy said.

"I don't know. My parents would never let me see such a movie. They won't let me go to a movie unless they see it first or know all about it," said Lilly.

"Oh Lilly, you are such a baby. Do you let your parents control everything you do?"

Lilly thought for a moment and then asked, "Do your parents know what you are doing? Do they think it is OK?"

"No, not exactly," said Krissy. "But, they say that I can do whatever I want as long as I don't hurt anyone or put myself in any danger. My father says you have to live for today and that I should just have fun."

"Gosh, that is not exactly what my folks say. They want me to listen to them and they often remind me of the 10 commandments. You know where God says to honor your mother and father. I guess I just think that is right," answered Lilly.

It sounds to me as if God just doesn't want you to have fun. Well, will you go or not? Make up your mind," said Krissy, more forcefully than before.

Lilly took a deep breath and finally said, "I think I better not -- because I am pretty sure I have to babysit for Gabby on Saturday. My folks are going to a Minnesota Twins baseball game with some friends. ... Oops, Mom's home now and I have to go. I'll talk to you later. See ya."

Making a Good Decision

Lilly looked at the phone as she closed it up and felt very confused. Just then, her mother came into the kitchen and asked, "Did you have a good day at school?"

"Yes, it was OK. We studied the founding of our country. Um... can I call Grandpa? I have some questions to ask him."

"What about?" asked Mom.

Lilly explains, "Grandpa and I have talked about why people view things differently, even though they have many things in common."

"Does this have anything to do with your friend, Krissy?" asked Mom.

"It is a little about Krissy. She has some strange ideas, and I'm not sure you would like them." said Lilly. Just then, there was a knock on the garage door.

"Oh, here comes Grandpa. I didn't have time to tell you that he was going to stop by and drop off Dad's plumbing tools. He looks happy; he must have fixed the leak," said Mom with a smile. "Let's talk about Krissy later."

"OK," said Lilly, as she ran to give Grandpa a hug.

"Hi, Grandpa; I'm so glad you're here. In fact, I was going to call you because I need to talk to you about something that is bothering me."

"Sure, Lilly, you know I always love talking to one of my sweet granddaughters. What's up?" asked Grandpa.

Lilly started, "Remember when you were telling me how people view things differently; how they have different ideas according to how they think."

Grandpa scratched his head, trying to remember, and finally said, "Ah, yes I do. We talked about how they had different views, and I called them 'worldviews.' We said each worldview is based on a belief system that determines how we look at the world and events."

Lilly agreed, "Yes, that's it. You said all the facts and evidence were the same for both views, but our personal worldview determines our conclusions. Someone with a Christian worldview would say that God created the earth while someone who doesn't believe in God would look for another explanation. Both require faith because no one has actually observed the earth's creation, nor can we redo it in a laboratory. "

"You remember it well -- but why are you asking me about it today?" asked Grandpa.

Wondering about Worldviews

"Well, I have a new situation concerning views. Oh, I mean worldviews. You and Grandma believe that Christianity played an important role in the founding of our country. But, Miss Webber, our teacher, does not have that view. We studied the founding of our country today, and Christianity wasn't even mentioned – not by Miss Webber or anywhere in the text book. My friend, Krissy, says the reason we don't study it is because it is not important and not even true. Which view is true? I don't understand," said Lilly.

Grandpa said, "Lilly, let's try to sort out your confusion. But, before we do, let's go back to the time when our country was being established and our Constitution was being written. That time was the founding era and we need to understand what was happening both in Europe and in the colonies then.

Our Founding Fathers held fast to a Biblical worldview, but in Europe a different view was emerging. This period was called "the Enlightenment" or "the age of reason." Both of these views (Biblical and Enlightenment) had some common goals. They both held a high value to life, liberty, education, science, good government, morality, etc. However, they differed dramatically in their foundation. Some of the philosophers of the Enlightenment era were also strong Christians, and they used Scripture to determine truth. Others denied God and said He was not involved in day-to-day events. Those who denied God created the man-centered worldview. It's called 'secular humanism.' It is still around today and we see it in people who live for the here and now," said Grandpa.

"Oh, that sounds like Krissy's dad's worldview," said Lilly.

"That could be. Many have it. Another thing to know about the enlightenment worldview is it holds that man is 'good' and can solve all problems through reasoning. Truth is not important or based on Scripture but on man's desires.

"The Biblical worldview holds that the Bible is God's living word and the basis of truth. And that through His Son, Jesus Christ, He provides for all our needs. Lilly, remember when Jesus taught us the Lord's prayer. He said **'Your kingdom come, your will be done on earth as it is in heaven.'"** (Matthew 6:10)

Lilly said, "Yes, I remember that part."

Grandpa went on, "When He said 'Your will be done,' it means whatever God "wills" will be done. Here, we see God's sovereign power at work. Lilly, sovereign means God is over all things. So, Lilly how would you compare both worldviews?"

Lilly thought awhile and then said, "Grandpa, the difference is whether a person thinks God is in charge -- or man is."

Grandpa reached his hand out and said, "Good job! Give me five!" And they both laughed.

Lilly responded, "OK, things are starting to make sense. I wasn't sure about what you meant by a foundation for each view. It seems we have a God-centered foundation or a man-centered foundation."

"Lilly, I'm proud of you! Let's take this a bit farther. Let's find out what Scripture has to say about different views. Would you get me your Bible or your family Bible?" asked Grandpa.

Searching the Scriptures

Lilly ran up to her room and soon returned with her Bible. Grandpa opened it up and started to read, **"See to it that no one takes you captive through hollow and deceptive philosophy, which depends on human tradition and the basic principles of this world rather than on Christ."** (Colossians 2:8). Lilly, this is so important.

Here's another reference: **"Timothy, guard what has been entrusted to your care. Turn away from godless chatter and the opposing ideas of what is falsely called knowledge ..."** (1 Timothy 6:20). Lilly, these Biblical passages were written over 2,000 years ago and they still apply today. What do you think they mean?"

Lilly thought awhile and then answered, "Grandpa, it sounds as if God is telling us that people fall for lies."

Grandpa said, "Well, you could say that -- and in many cases it would be true, because many people have been unknowingly deceived, or at least misled. Let's read from 1 Thessalonians 5:21-22: **"Test everything. Hold on to the good. Avoid every kind of evil."** What do you think that means?"

Be Careful and Know God as Your Guide

Lilly said, "I think God is saying be very careful about what you read and hear, and ask a lot of questions to find out the real answer. And most of all, use God's word as your guide."

Grandpa said, "Lilly, that's right -- but what about the second part about doing good and abstaining from evil?"

Lilly explained, "I think it means that by using the Bible, we can know what is good and right, and we can do what is right in God's plan. That is different from what my friend, Krissy, thinks. She wants to do whatever feels right to her."

Grandpa said, "Lilly, I'm not sure I understand what you're saying about your friend. "

Lilly said,"That's OK, Grandpa. I need to talk to Mom about her."

"OK, Lilly," Grandpa continued. "Back to your point that our Christian heritage was left out of your textbook. Based on our discussion today, and on the truth about our Founding Fathers, we know that Christianity was influential in the founding of our country. Do you agree?"

Lilly said," Sure -- because you say so. "

"Lilly, I appreciate that, but it's not good enough. I know you trust me, but you need to verify the truth for yourself. Let's look at some facts. In the Declaration of Independence, God is mentioned four times. If that is true, why would your textbooks ignore God's influence?"

Finding the Facts

Lilly paused and then responded, "Just a minute, Grandpa;

I'll be right back." She soon returned with a copy of the Declaration of Independence that Grandma gave her. "OK, Grandpa, I am going to check this out for myself. "Let's see," she said as she scanned the document …

"Yes! There are four! It refers to:
1. Nature's God
2. Endowed by their Creator
3. Appealing to the Supreme Judge of the World
4. Reliance on the protection of divine Providence.

Those four things -- they all mean God!"

Desiring Discernment

Grandpa explained, "Yes, Christianity certainly influenced the signers of this heritage document. Lilly, you passed the test! You know, God has given you the gift of discernment."

"Grandpa, that's a big word. What does discernment mean?"

Grandpa responded, "You already have shown me through your questions and actions that you want to know the truth. You went to the Declaration of Independence to find the answers. You have a discerning attitude, which means you carefully check things out and search for the truth. I think it is a very admirable gift from God -- and you should praise and thank Him for it."

Lilly smiled up at Grandpa, gratefully.

Laws contrary to the Bible are not acceptable

"OK, let's finish this lesson," said Grandpa. "More than a hundred years ago, educators with an Enlightenment worldview started to leave our Christian heritage out of the text books because their view holds that God does not exist or that He only plays a minor role in everyday life. They are omitting an important piece of history, which is a form of deception. God's verse on 'empty deception' can apply to leaving things out. Soon teachers, parents and even the church left the Christian heritage out and it was forgotten completely! Once forgotten, the next step is to say it never happened at all. And so, the Krissys of the world never do learn complete history. They are never taught what our Founding Fathers knew – that no law is valid if contrary to the law of God."

Lilly pondered this for a moment and then asked, "Why do those people—you called them educators—get to write it rather than a person like you with a Biblical worldview?"

Grandpa answered, "That's a very good question. Over a period of time, more people holding that view have become more influential in our education system. They now control what is included in our history books."

Lilly asked, "So why wouldn't they let both views be written? After all, you said before, that we have several common ideas, like liberty and education."

Grandpa explained, "That's a good question, Lilly. It's sad, because they should. Some folks who have a Biblical worldview want to change things, but they are afraid. There is a strong lobby to keep anything remotely honoring to Christianity out of the educational system. Some people have even lost their jobs because of their worldview."

Lilly said, "That's not fair. Isn't that what liberty and freedom of speech is all about?

"Yes," Grandpa said sadly.

"Remember Lilly, this is the same as not letting God's creation into science books as an equal view of our origins. Maybe they are afraid of the truth or don't know the truth. Remember what Jesus said, **"If you hold to my teaching, you are really my disciples. Then you will know the truth, and the truth will set you free."** (John 8:31b-32). I hope this helps you understand what is happening. Let's keep talking the truth, and praying that God would make His truth clear to us and to everyone."

Lilly gave Grandpa a big hug, saying, "Thanks Grandpa. I'm sure lucky that I can talk to you. Now, I need to talk to Mom and Dad."

When Lilly went into the house, Mom was peeling potatoes at the sink. "Mom, I don't think I want to spend much time with Krissy anymore. She wants me to go to this movie …"

Fun Fact!

To truly appreciate our Christian Heritage, plan a trip to Washington D.C. and view all the glorious sculptures and paintings that depict our country's reliance upon God.

Or—do some web research and see what you can find!

Part I

Stepping Back In Time: Personal Stories

1613:
Pocahontas - A Christian Sister

In 1607, Englishmen arrived in Jamestown and started the first Virginia settlement in the new world. They endured many struggles as they began to build a new life in a raw and dangerous environment. One of their first acts was to build a large wooden cross on the shore. Reverend Robert Hunt said they were to bring religion to all who lived in darkness.

One of the settlers was John Smith, a rather arrogant man that some called a troublemaker. Soon after his arrival in Virginia, Smith was captured by Indian braves. His ego and fast-talking somehow convinced the great tribal chief, Powhatan, to set him free and even allowed him to take corn back to Jamestown. That was a gift to all those at the settlement, because they were out of food.

Another time when John Smith was captured, Pocahontas is said to have saved his life. She was the daughter of Powhatan, the Indian sachem or chief, and lived near the Jamestown settlement. The Indians were about to kill Smith but she lay down beside him and pleaded for mercy, and her father, the chief, listened. We don't know if the story is really true or not. The first few writings by Smith never mentioned it. Only later, after she became well known, did Smith include this story in his writings.

The saga of Pocahontas continues—she was sold by some Indians to an English sea captain who took her to Jamestown where she was held for ransom. Her father, Powhatan, paid the bushels of corn stipulated, but his daughter was not released. This resulted in an ugly confrontation.

Meanwhile, Pocahontas was being educated and instructed in the Christian faith and becoming a true believer. She fell in love with John Rolfe, who asked her father for her hand in marriage. It seemed to be divine providence and a perfect way to make peace between the two groups. They all gathered for the wedding celebration and the Indians generously brought an abundance of food. This provided a feast for the Virginia settlers, but more importantly, it provided peace until Powhatan's death.

In 1616, at the request of the Queen, Pocahontas, her husband, and their son, Thomas, traveled to England where they were treated like royalty. Sadly, while in England, she contracted pneumonia and died. Her son returned to Virginia, married and many of his (and Pocahontas') descendents became prominent in both government and business.

Why is it important to remember Pocahontas as part of our Christian heritage? She was one of the first Native Americans to be baptized into the Christian faith. She accepted Christ and became a new creation, from 2 Corinthians 5:17, **"Therefore, if anyone is in Christ, he is a new creation; the old has gone, the new has come."** As was customary at that time, she took a new name at her baptism: the Biblical name, Rebecka.

Disney made a cartoon film of Pocahontas, but unfortunately, the film communicated her history inaccurately. In the film, Pocahontas married John Smith and converted him to pagan spiritualism which is fantasy and not true. Her real life and her Christian faith are never mentioned.

There is a large, beautiful oil painting of Pocahontas that hangs on the wall of the main rotunda of the U.S. Capital which commemorates her 1613 Christian baptism.

Peter Marshall and David Manuel, *The Light and the Glory*, chapter 4

1620:
Olivia's Story of the Mayflower

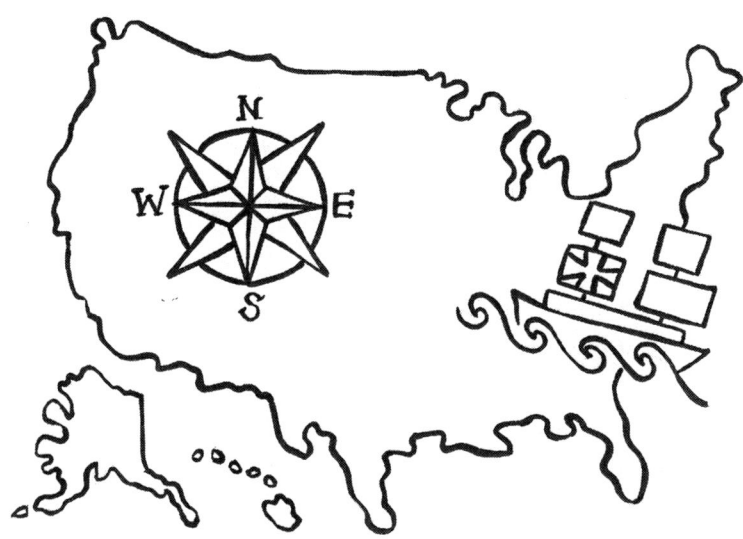

Memory Verses
- Mark 16:15 – *"He said to them, "Go into all the world and preach the good news to all creation."*

Meet Olivia and listen as she visits the Mayflower and reminisces about being aboard the ship some 30 years earlier when it landed at Plymouth Rock.

Welcome! I did not see you sitting there! I am deep in thought and memories. I should introduce myself. My name is Olivia, and when I was just 13, my mom, dad, brother and I sailed here to Plymouth on this ship, the Mayflower. Oh, that was such an eventful time!

Look here and see this ship. It is old now for it was 30 years ago, in 1620, that it brought us, the Pilgrims, here to the New World. Today, I came just to see the Mayflower one more time. Look there, it's the mast that cracked ... but I am getting ahead of myself.

This is a story of adventure and trust in God, for we acted out the great commission, a command that our Lord Jesus gave to his disciples when he returned after his resurrection. He told the disciples in Mark 16:15 - **"Go into all the world and preach the gospel to every creature."** That is what Jesus commanded us to do -- and that is exactly what we did.

From Smelly Alley to ... America!

Now, let me tell you my story. I was born in England but moved to Holland when I was one and lived in what was called "Smelly Alley." I am sure you can imagine what that means! Would you like to live there? It was near the waterfront and not in the best part of town.

My parents and other Separatists had escaped from England in order to worship God according to the Bible. In England, we endured many hardships and deaths at the hands of King James and his brutes and even some of those in the church were hostile to us. Sometimes, people do terrible and mean things, saying they are doing it for the church or for Christianity, but really they are just using the church or the name of Jesus to do what they want. We must read the Bible to really understand what God would have us do.

While in Holland, my brother was born and all seemed to be going well. We had a small house in a small village, and everyone worked very hard. We were allowed to worship as we wished. However, we weren't able to talk about our faith openly and, of course, our school did not teach anything about Christianity. We had years of religious freedom to worship our Lord but could not advance the principles of the gospel.

Religious Freedom is Essential

Then one day, my father and mother were quite excited. They had been attending a lot of meetings, so my brother, Ryan, and I knew something was up. I heard in school that Spain might invade Holland and our religious freedom would once again be taken from us. My parents were also very upset because so many of the children were becoming more like the Dutch and less like our community of Separatists. (At that time, we were called Separatists, but later we were called Pilgrims.) We wanted a place where our community would be safe from immoral influences, so we could follow Scripture.

One day, my father said we might be going to a place he called "the New World." My brother was excited, and I was scared. I did not want to leave my friends. However, we had always been taught to obey God's word and our parents, and to trust in God. We learned this in Philippians 4:6, **"Do not be anxious about anything, but in everything, by prayer and petition, with thanksgiving, present your requests to God."** So we waited and waited.

In our church community, we had wonderful leaders like Pastor John Robinson and William Bradford. Pastor Robinson was our leader, and he always relied on prayer. Mr. Bradford had given up a fortune in England to be part of our community because he would pay taxes to the king, but kneel only to Jesus Christ. He was only 17 years old when he joined our community. Before any meeting, we always prayed first.

"Good riddance" Becomes a Blessing

Father was very concerned because we needed two things in order to sail. We needed a land grant from King James, but he hated us. Second, we needed enough money to pay for a ship. Surprisingly, King James did give us a land grant and permission to settle on property in the New World. It is believed that he said," Good riddance." So, one problem was solved.

Then some adventurers, people who wanted to invest in the New World, paid for our crossing. It was agreed that we would work for them for seven years after our arrival in the New World. I suppose we were slaves to them and their company, but we knew we could worship God and live out Christ's great commission. We learned this in Matthew 28:19, "Therefore go and make disciples of all nations..."

The Voyage

Only half of our community agreed to go on the first ship. My father and mother signed up to go. I was both proud and scared. It would be exciting. I knew that many ships never survived the trip, and there was a great chance of illness. Then too, I had heard about a terrible sour lemon drink one needed to drink in order to prevent scurvy, a horrible disease sailors contracted for lack of vitamin C. I used to pray, "Dear God, give me courage and make me strong so that I can help to keep your word."

We read John Smith's book *A Description of New England*. The New World sounded like paradise, but father kept cautioning us and reminding us that God's plan was most important. Later, we found out that much of John Smith's book was really a lie.

First, we started out in a ship called the Speedwell, but it leaked. After trying twice to leave port, we were put on the Mayflower, a much bigger sailing ship -- it weighed 180 tons! The Mayflower was called a sweet ship because it never carried smelly fish cargo.

"Strangers," the name given to those who were not part of our community, were on the Mayflower with us. They were sailing to the New World for a better life, not necessarily for religious reasons. They were people like John Alden, a young man who wanted to go to America to work as a cooper. That meant he wanted to make barrels, tubs and casks. Myles Standish was a short man with a sword who wanted to defend the new colony. All total, there were 102 of us.

Before we finally left, Pastor John Robinson ordered a time of fasting and prayer. Trusting in God was most important. We still call for days of fasting and prayer; God honors our needs. We did not pray for ill health for King James, but I was glad we weren't under his control. We would be FREEEE!

The first part of the trip was rather uneventful. The crew was very unpleasant, and they had a way of punishing and making fun of us. We ate a kind of cracker bread the sailors called hard tack, as well as salt pork, dried fruits and vegetables, and lemon juice. Often, we even had to pick bugs out of our food, which was really very unpleasant.

Mayflower Highlights

Four big events happened while on the Mayflower.

1. First, we were in a terrible storm. I was sure we were all going to perish. The water came over the edge of the ship. Of course, we had to be down in the hold and I hung on to my brother and prayed and prayed. All of a sudden, we heard a large cracking sound as the main beam cracked and the mast fell. The captain and crew just looked at it with grim faces, trying to decide whether to continue on or turn around. Then one of the Pilgrims remembered that he brought a large iron construction screw on the voyage. They used it to raise the beam into place. The repair worked! After that, most of the crew left us alone -- and even sometimes asked about our God.

2. However, one crew member still was nasty. He used to snarl at us, call us names, and said half of us would never make it to the New World. "Soon as ye die, I will find your belongings and they will be mine. God can't protect you." We were all afraid of him. One day, suddenly, he was hit by a terrible illness and died. We had a Christian burial at sea for him, and we all prayed for his soul. We also had a second burial at sea -- a young manservant of Dr. Fuller. The crew saw these things as a sign and no longer treated us poorly.

3. The third big event was the birth of Mr. and Mrs. Hopkins' baby. They named him Oceanus. Dr. Fuller, a Pilgrim, was on board and he helped deliver the baby. God was good, even though we had little food and often felt hungry.

4. The best event of the voyage was when, after 66 days of travel, we started to see driftwood. We knew we were near land, but we were not near the Hudson River where we had the land grant. We were far up the coast, and try as we might, we could not go south. It was hard for our captain to know what he should do. It was finally decided to take a small boat to shore. It was kind of like when Moses sent Joshua into the new land to look around! Several went to explore and they came back with food and stories of an abandoned village with buried yellow seeds, which one of the sailors called corn.

Of course, we all knew that it was too late into the year to plant any food, so the corn was a real gift from God. We had to ration all our food and often, we were hungry. An abandoned

Indian village provided us a cleared area to begin building shelters and start a community, which we named Plymouth.

Making Laws and Choosing Leaders

Since we were not on the land the king had granted us, we were not under any laws or government. Without any organization, there would be lawlessness and everyone working and living only for oneself. What to do? The debate was powerful. The strangers who were not part of our community were afraid that if we were in control, they would have to worship as we did. However, they also realized the need for laws and organization.

Finally, the adults all decided to make laws and choose the leaders to rule this new community the same way the Pilgrims chose their church leaders. Every man who was head of a household voted as a family representative, thereby affecting the common good of us all. It was an efficient system, and my dad represented our family. Each family wrote down their ideas and then everyone discussed them. After much work, the Mayflower Compact was written and signed. This allowed men and women to live under rules of their own making, rather than the dictates of a king.

This agreement, the Mayflower Compact, stated that **each person would do his or her best to do God's will and protect the rights of others.** This document secured the right of all people to worship God and live in peace with their neighbors. Plymouth was the birthplace of true liberty. **Liberty is not the right to live as we please, but the power and responsibility to live as God requires.**

The Compact also stated plainly why we had come to the New World. Let me read to you the exact reasons **"...for the glory of God and advancement of the Christian faith."**

Our first act was the election of John Carver to be governor for a year. The next year, Carver left office and William Bradford became governor and remained governor for many, many years. We named the new settlement Plymouth, after the town in England from which we sailed. It was very exciting, but we were still very scared.

So we lived out God's great commission to go into the world and preach the gospel to every creature. My father said it was a big church "relocation project" that worked and had wonderful consequences!

The first year in the New World was very difficult. Both my brother and my mom died of a severe illness, but living conditions did get better. Now our community is alive with the love of the Lord.

Well, dear friends, it is time for me to go. I must draw some water and make some new candles for our little house. I am glad I was able to tell you my story. Remember to live by God's word and to trust in the Lord.

Accounts from: William Bradford, *Of Plymouth Plantation*
The Vision Forum, Inc. Bulverde, Texas
More information regarding the Mayflower Compact on page 89.
Note: Olivia is a fictitious character but the events are factual.

1621:
Squanto – A Christian Brother

The first winter was difficult for the Pilgrims, and they were anxious for warm weather and better hunting. One day in late spring, there was great excitement when a tall, muscular Indian who spoke English walked into their settlement.

The Indian's name was Samoset. He was from the northern Algonquin tribe and had sailed down the coast with Captain Dermer, an English sea captain, who taught him the English language.

Samoset was able to answer many questions. He told the Pilgrims that until 1617, a large hostile tribe of natives called the Patuxet lived on the cleared property that the Pilgrims had settled. Not too many years before, they had all disappeared -- possibly from some disease. Now, neighboring tribes were afraid of the area because of the fear of a supernatural spirit.

The following week, Samoset returned to Plymouth with Squanto, another Indian who also spoke English. He was of the Patuxet tribe and was now a brother in Christ.

In 1605, he was captured by adventurers and taken to England as a slave. After nine years in captivity, he escaped and tried to return to his native land with a man named Captain Hunt. However, the ship captain tricked Squanto and took him to Spain, where he was sold to a monastery. Before long, the monks shared their faith with Squanto, and he became a believer in Jesus. The monks arranged for him to return to London and travel across the ocean to his Patuxet home with Captain Dermer. Squanto soon learned that all his family and tribesmen were gone. He was without a family, so he elected to remain with his new Christians friends, which was a benefit to all.

Soon after Squanto arrived, the neighboring Wampanoag's chief, Massasoit, and sixty painted warriors came to the settlement. The Pilgrims were scared, but they treated them with hospitality and respect. (They showed them the love of Christ.) This pleased the chief, and by the time the meeting was over, they entered into a peace agreement.

God continued to watch over the Pilgrims. He had given them a safe voyage, a place to start their settlement, and now, friends to help them. Squanto taught the Pilgrims how to grow corn, hunt various animals, cook the natural berries and vegetables of the area and even taught them about the use of herbs for medicine. Governor Bradford wrote in his journal that Squanto was a true gift from God.

The First Thanksgiving

The first Thanksgiving was declared by Governor William Bradford in Plymouth, Massachusetts in October 1621. He proclaimed, *"All ye Pilgrims with your wives and little ones, do gather at the meeting house, on the hill... there to listen to the pastor and render thanksgiving to the Almighty God for all His blessings."*

1621: William Bradford - The Beginning of American Free Enterprise

Memory Verse
- Genesis 2:15 – **"The LORD God took the man and put him in the Garden of Eden to work it and take care of it."**

William Bradford was elected the governor of Plymouth Plantation in 1621, one year after the Pilgrims arrived in the New World. His diary, *Of Plymouth Plantation*, tells not only of the courage and difficulty the Pilgrims had in getting to the New World but of their struggles and successes as they implemented Biblical teachings in everyday life. Reading Bradford's diary gives one a new appreciation of the people who gave America the Christian foundation which has given people freedom and prosperity.

Soon after arriving in the new world it became very obvious that the pilgrims form of community living with shared production was not working. There was little motivation to work when all the fruits of one's labor were shared equally.

"Communal farming with no individual incentive does not even work with Christians who have common vision, goals and purposes. The Pilgrims gave us this example in the first two years in America. Compelled by the contract with their financial backers, the Pilgrims farmed the land communally. The lack of incentive to work resulted in such a poor crop that the Pilgrims almost starved during the first two winters. To alleviate this problem, the leaders shifted to an individual enterprise system where every family farmed their own parcel of land, and ate the fruit of their own labor. In his *Of Plymouth Plantation*, Governor Bradford wrote, 'This had very good success; for it made all hands very industrious... The women now went willingly into the field, and took their little ones with them to set corn, which before would allege weakness, and inability; whom to have compelled would have been thought great tyranny and oppression.'[1] They produced an abundant crop and never lacked for food again." [2]

Each family was given a plot of land to farm. It gave all, even those with indentured servants, the incentive to work and be productive. Larger crops and more goods made it easier to help and provide for those who could not work. They shared out of their abundance, even with the newcomers.

[1] William Bradford, *Of Plymouth Plantation* (Boston 1901), p 162
[2] Mark Beliles and Stephen McDowell, *America's Providential History*, p 201

Of Plymouth Plantation
William Bradford's diary from 1647

"But about ye 16 of March, a certaine Indian came bouldly amongst them, and spoke to them in broken English, which they could well understand, but marveled at it ... He would tell them also of another Indian whose name was Squanto, a native of this place, who had been in England & could speake better English then him selfe.

"Afterwards they (as many as able) began to plant ther corne, in which servise Squanto stood them in great stead, showing them both ye maner how to set it, and after how to dress and tend it ...

"And thus they found ye Lord to be with them in all their ways, and to blesse their outgoings and incomings, for which let his holy name have ye praise for ever, to all posteritie."

[2] Mark Beliles and Stephen McDowell, *America's Providential History*, p 73

Part II

Learn From Family Stories & Conversation

God's Hand on the Newcomers

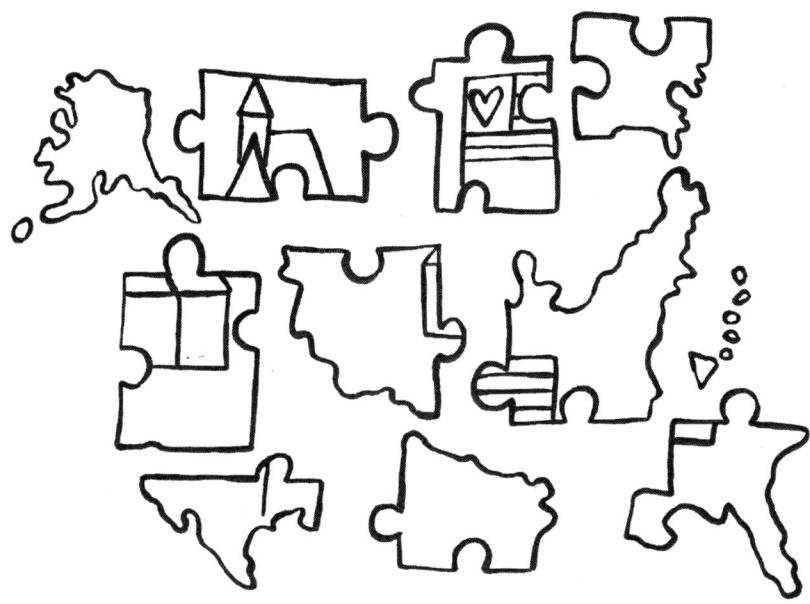

Memory Verses
- Leviticus 19:18 – *"Do not seek revenge or bear a grudge against one of your people, but love your neighbor as yourself..."*
- John 13:34 – *"A new command I give you: Love one another. As I have loved you, so you must love one another."*

It was a beautiful August evening when the Olsen family finished setting up their tent for a weekend of enjoying nature at the Lake Owen campground. Dad, Eric and Greg found just the right logs to start the fire, while Mom and Cindy started getting things ready for s'mores.

"Wow, this is fun! Camping is awesome! Look at the stars. It's wild," said Greg, as he added one more log to the fire.

"Yes, I love this, too," said Mom as she gazed into the night sky. "I like being away from carpools and all the activities. God really created a beautiful earth and especially, a beautiful north woods. It makes me think of Psalm 19: **'The heavens declare the glory of God.'** Nature shows all of us the complexity of God's beautiful creation."

"Well, I miss all the things I have at home—like a bathroom, our Wii, the TV and my friends. I also forgot Kit, my American Girl Doll, and I miss her," said Cindy sadly, as she looked one more time for the forgotten doll.

"Look what I have for you—a slingshot," said Dad, excitedly. "We can try it out tomorrow and line up tin cans and see if we can hit them. You know, the Pilgrims and early founders of this country used slingshots for hunting game. They needed to hunt their own food with only the simplest tools."

He was examining the slingshot and pretending to load and shoot it. "Tomorrow, we will see if we can become as accurate as the Pilgrims. Cindy, aren't you studying the colonists in American history?"

"Yes, but we aren't studying about slingshots. We did read about their way of life and that they gave up a lot of comforts when they came to America. They lived like we are, in the woods, with no electricity or running water," she said, with a little pout in her voice.

"That's right," answered Mom. "But they were lucky in that they had a real purpose for traveling to the New World and starting a new home. They wanted to spread the teachings of Jesus Christ, to worship God, and raise a family in freedom."

"Well, didn't they just go to church on Sunday like we do?" asked Cindy.

"Not exactly," answered Dad. "There is so much to tell you about the founders of this country -- their sacrifices, their determination, and their desire to live Christian lives. It is called our Christian heritage. Besides the Pilgrims, have you ever heard of the Quakers or the Puritans? They were also Christians who came to the New World with one primary reason, to spread Christianity and worship in freedom. Many left England because of the intense persecution of believers by King James I. And some fled Europe because of a new philosophy called Enlightenment that was becoming very popular and was not always based on God's Word.

Christian consensus

"The newcomers to America were of different Christian denominations, such as Presbyterian, Methodist, Lutherans, and Catholics and they were from different countries: Germany, England, Scotland, France and Spain. The three million – plus -- people living in the colonies at the time of the Revolutionary War shared what was called a Christian consensus. Their thinking and philosophy was based on the Bible. We know this because they wrote many documents that have been preserved and studied.[1]

"Now, back to your questions. No, they didn't have electricity, computers, cell phones, television, radio, or running water. They got along with very little in the way of physical comforts. They did worship God on Sunday by gathering together for church, but they believed it was important to follow the teachings of the Bible all through the week. They used the Bible as their textbook for life. They lived their lives based on the 10 Commandments and the two great commissions."

"I had to memorize the two great commissions for Wednesday Night Group. Want me to tell you?" asked Greg.

"Yes," everyone answered in unison.

Greg answered with great pride and a smile on his face. "John 13:34... **"Love one another. As I have loved you..."** And Matthew 28:19: **"Go and make disciples of all nations, baptizing them in the name of the Father and of the Son and of the Holy Spirit ..."**

"Bravo! That was great, Greg!" exclaimed Dad.

"Oh, he's just showing off... I wish we could know more about the Puritans and Quakers. Can we search them on the internet?" asked Cindy.

"Sure," said Dad. "Let's use the wireless access from the Ranger station. I guess we're not quite as primitive as the early Pilgrims or settlers! Technology certainly is amazing ... it's one of God's gifts to us."

Eric did a computer search on Quakers and found some great information. "Look, here is video clip of a Puritan on YouTube!'" The family leaned closer to see the reenactment on the computer screen.

The Puritans

In the video, a Puritan man in authentic costume began: "I know much about this group of which you speak, for I am a Puritan. Let me tell you about my community.

Many of us left England in the 1600s for the New World called America. We left because we could no longer worship in the apostate Anglican Church of England, which did not follow the Covenant Way. They did not honor an agreement between God and His people.

Originally, we stayed in England, thinking we could purify the church, which is how we got the name Puritans. A small group known as the Separatists had gone to the New World years before, and they were known as Pilgrims.

We stayed in England -- until the discrimination and killing became too much. The very church we wanted to purify was turning against us, which caused many of us to leave for the New World. That was a miracle in itself for the king did not want us to leave and he would not give the Massachusetts Bay Colony a charter. However, he accidentally signed the charter without reading it.

Reverend John Winthrop, the best-known Puritan, was to be the governor in this new colony. However, he was not with the first settlers and when he arrived one year later, he was amazed to see the deplorable health, living, and eating conditions. The colonist didn't have any direction and were rather lazy, each expecting others to do the work. Rev. Winthrop would not stand for this behavior. He said. **"By God's grace, everyone is going to have a proper dwelling place and all are going to do their share of the work, even those who had brought over servants to do their work."** He used the following verse to remind the community that they needed to work together: **"Love your neighbor as yourself."** Leviticus 19:18 [2]

The Pilgrims taught us about individual liberty and free enterprise. We taught them about living under God's rule, encouraging repentance not punishment. Man is born sinful and so we gave people the right to ask forgiveness of God and anyone that they had injured. We were overzealous and had made laws requiring all to join and participate in the church which, by its very nature, stifled liberty.

However, we did not follow the rule of repentance when, in 1692, we overstepped God's plan and tried, convicted and executed 20 people for witchcraft. This was stopped quickly and many of those responsible for the executions repented for their sinful acts. Hundreds of executions were done in Europe.

Little did we know that in the future (the 20th and 21st century), we Puritans would be categorized as sour, gloomy, severe and mean-spirited. Much of this information would come from fictional stories that will mislead and be inaccurate. Up until then, the Puritans were honored and respected for their hard work, discipline, compassion, community sharing, and their willingness to examine their own motives and behavior.

We would be known as excellent parents because we used discipline and taught our children to respect others. [3]

"Now, what do you think of the Puritans?" asked Dad.

Greg, Eric and Cindy looked surprised. Greg answered, "Sounds like most people have the wrong idea about the Puritans today. It's good to know the truth – that they were known for being hard working, disciplined, compassionate, and willing to share with their community."

"Yes," said Dad. "Those are great qualities for us to consider. Now, let's see what we can find about the Quakers."

Cindy began a computer search on Quakers and found some great information: "Oh look, here's a Quaker story for us to share."

The Quakers

My name is Jonathan Penn, and I am a member of the Friends Society of Quakers. I am a Quaker and I live in Penn's Woods. I hear tell that some say this land will eventually be called Pennsylvania.

We came from England, where we were persecuted for teaching from the Holy Bible. In fact, our leader William Penn, my great uncle, was imprisoned three times in the Tower of London. He dreamed of going to the new world and starting a new colony. He was fortunate that the king owed his family a large sum of money. He bargained with the king and exchanged it for a large track of land in the New World.

We all came over on the ship called Welcome and landed in 1681. The Pilgrims had already been here for almost 60 years and the Puritans, for 40 years. Mr. Penn paid the king for the new land but knew that the Indians owned it, so he called the Indians together and offered to buy the property a second time at a fair price. The Indians accepted and the Quakers and Indians lived in peace. (Note: There is an original painting of this event of 1682 in the Rotunda of the U.S. Capital in Washington D.C.)

William Penn loved to read the Psalms and wanted to bring brotherly love to the new colony. He gave Philadelphia the motto, "City of Brotherly Love" because of the Quaker compassion for others.

In 1682, Mr. Penn wrote "the Charter of Liberties" which cited from Scripture that government was to terrify evildoers and cherish those who do well. (Romans 13:1-5). He wrote to Peter the Great, Czar of Russia, and said, **"Those who will not be governed by God will be ruled by tyrants."** [4]

Mr. Penn has given all citizens of the colony freedom of religion and protection for all religions. He also added language to our charter which stated that only citizens who acknowledged Almighty God as Creator would be able to serve in the new government.

He said, "All persons having children shall cause such to be instructed in reading and writing, so that they may be able to read the Scriptures and to write by the time they attain 12 years of age."[5] The other colonies are also mandating that teaching be done for all children. In Massachusetts, a law was passed called the "Old Deluder Satan Act" which was to help all children learn Scripture so Satan could not deceive them.

Right now, things are very simple. We live in a log cabin that is very nice. The idea of log cabins came from Swedish immigrants who live close by. The cabin is an amazing structure and can be made with the materials found in the nearby forests.

We do our own work. Quakers are known for hard work, and we try to make life better for each other. We are happy and in awe of this new Israel.

"History is exciting and interesting. We can learn great things from the past. But I think that's enough for today," Mom said. As she turned off the computer, she said, "Now, who would like a s'more? Let's enjoy God's beautiful natural surroundings."

"Me!" chimed everyone.

[1] Tim LaHaye, *Faith of Our Founding Fathers*, p 33
[2] Peter Marshall, *The Glory and the Light*, p 165
[3] Peter Marshall, *The Glory and the Light*, chapter 9
[4] William Federer, *America's God & Country*, p 500
[5] William Federer, *America's God & Country*, p 499

Cough Medicine from the 1700s

Take 30 garden snails and 30 earth worms of middling size, bruise ye snails and wash them and ye worms in fair water, cut ye worms in pieces. Boil these in a quart of spring water to a pint. Pour it boiling hot on 2 ounces of candied Eringo root, sliced thin. When it is cold, strain it thro' a flannel bag. Take a quarter of a pint of it warm water, with an equal quantity of cow's milk. Continue this course till well.

From the receipt book of Mrs. Ann Blencowe, dated 1694, as recorded in *Colonial Kids*, Laurie Carlson, 1952

A Nation of Prayer

Memory Verses
- Matthew 10:29-31 – *"Are not two sparrows sold for a penny? Yet not one of them will fall to the ground apart from the will of your Father. And even the very hairs of your head are all numbered. So don't be afraid; you are worth more than many sparrows."*
- Psalms 127:1 – *"... Unless the LORD builds the house, its builders labor in vain. Unless the LORD watches over the city, the watchmen stand guard in vain."*

On a windy but warm day, the Brekke family was busy settling into a wonderful north woods cabin on Madeline Island on Lake Superior. Mother was just unpacking the last duffle bag and Keenan was sorting videos when Aidan came walking up to the porch. He was wearing his baseball mitt and was tossing a baseball as high into the air as he could.

Mother smiled at him and said, "This will be so much fun being on vacation with just our family and away from all the "business" of home. I love being with just the five of us for a time together. Not even my iPhone® works way up here!"

"Well, it may be fun for you, but I think it's dull. Finn is being a jerk -- he is not cooperating at all. I wish I had a brother my age, not a younger brother," sighed Aidan. "We are trying to make up a game for just the two of us. You know, new rules for just two players. I think it is only fair that we each have two 'outs.' But Finn thinks he should have three 'outs' just because he's younger and because he's not as strong as I am. I wish Drew and Dolan were here so we could have a real game. I have it all figured out, and it should be two outs, the same for each of us." With that Aidan collapsed into a swivel chair and soon ended up on the floor. Finn entered the room and snickered at his big brother on the floor.

"Mom, Aidan is not being fair," sighed Finn, with a very exasperated voice. "I want to play ball, but I am not as big or strong as he is. I need three outs and I want to be up first because I am smaller. He just doesn't understand."

"No, you don't understand. It is not my problem that you are smaller," said Aidan.

"I can't help it that I am smaller. You're not being fair! I wish we could forget baseball and find a place to ride our ripsticks," moaned Finn.

With that, Mother decided it was time to enter the noisy debate. "Hey, wait just a minute, it sounds to me like you are not getting anywhere in deciding new rules. You each have your own ideas and your own abilities. Aidan, you are older and stronger, and Finn, you are younger and not quite as strong. I assume both of you want the game to be fair, but you each are more concerned about yourself. Any ideas how we can solve this?"

"Yes, let's do it the way I want," said Aidan with a frown.

Ask God to Show us a Better Way

"Hmmm ... I think I have a better idea. Maybe we should

take some time out and ask God to show us a better way," said Mother.

"You mean pray?" asked Finn.

"Yes, I do. God does answer prayer. In fact, remember when you were studying about the founding of our country? Well, the founders disagreed about the rules for a new nation, so they went to God in prayer. It was a lot like your problem. The big states wanted more representation in the legislature and the little states felt that was unfair. Sound familiar?" asked Mother.

"I remember studying history and how they decided on the number of representatives in Congress, but I never learned that prayer had any part in it," said Aidan.

"That's too bad, because prayer played a very important part in our American history. The people building our new nation went to God in prayer and asked for His providential hand. That just means they prayed to God for His help and guidance --and also thanked Him," she said.

The First Continental Congress

"In 1774, representatives of the colonies met for the first time, in what was called the First Continental Congress, to discuss and debate the difficult situation with England. It was a fearful time because the representatives had heard rumors of an attack on Boston by the English. They were undecided about how to handle King George. He was unfair and mean spirited, and he tried to rule them from across the ocean.

"When they gathered together, they could only agree on one thing – that they needed to begin deliberations with prayer. The very first decision was to ask a minister to come and pray for the congress and to ask God to give everyone discernment! The Reverend Jacob Duche', an Episcopal clergyman, led everyone in prayer. The prayer was very moving and lasted three hours. Can you imagine praying for three hours? Can you imagine politicians today praying for three hours for God's leadership and direction? One man said it was worth his five days of travel on horseback just to be part of the prayer time," said Mother.

"Finn, stop chasing the dog and come and listen, OK?" said Mother, a bit annoyed.

"In that same year, the Continental Congress repeatedly called for prayer and fasting. For example, in March 1776, they stated that it is their duty to '... publicly acknowledge the overruling providence of God.'[1]

Revolutionary War

"The Revolutionary War itself was amazing because it was a 'David verses Goliath' situation. England was so strong and powerful, and the colonies were small and disorganized. Here is where the providence of God intervened in several ways. Many times, weather made all the difference in giving the colonies the advantage in battle. Because of one such miraculous event, the Continental Congress asked for public prayer and thanksgiving. They called for prayer, 'to celebrate the praises of our Divine Benefactor.'[2]

"When freedom from England was won, they had to design a new government because the Articles of Confederation under which they were governed during the war were inadequate for the new country.

"A Constitutional Convention met in Philadelphia in 1787 to revise the Articles of Confederation, but in the end, they wrote a new Constitution. Each colony could send as many representatives as they wished, but each colony would have only one vote. At the very first session, it pleased everyone to elect George Washington as the president of the Convention. James Madison acted as the secretary, and later, he became known as the father of the U.S. Constitution.

"They gathered in Philadelphia in the summer of 1787. The weather was extremely hot and of course, they only had hand-held fans to help keep them cool. Many representatives came and went due to other obligations, because they had to pay for their own cost of living and expenses.

"They did quite well coming to an agreement on just how our new nation would operate. They all wanted a democratic republic or a representative government elected by the people that included checks and balances. On the three major issues of slavery, regulation of commerce and representation, a genuine compromise was needed.

Equal Representation
"Then, they ran into a BIG problem -- similar to your problem. The small colonies, like Finn, wanted to be given equal representation in congress while the big colonies such as New York, like Aidan, wanted an advantage because they were larger in size and population. It became a real battle, and neither side was going to give in to the other. Well, the debate continued and soon, delegates became angry and started to leave. Several ideas were offered to solve the problem, but they still couldn't agree. It was so miserable that Benjamin Franklin, at 81 years of age, spoke out.

"Franklin addressed 'Mr. President,' referring to George Washington, because he was the president of the Constitutional Convention. Franklin described the difficulties and the successful progress that had been made in writing the Constitution. He mentioned how they had looked to other governments and to ancient history but found only imperfection and nothing suitable for the U.S. Constitution.

"Considering the great difficulty they were having, he asked why they had not humbly asked God to enlighten them. After all, in the beginning of the struggles with England, they had daily prayer in that very room to ask God for divine protection!

Their prayers were heard and were graciously answered. Frequently, God's hand was seen in the victorious struggle with England, allowing for the opportunity to create a new nation. Had they forgotten this powerful Friend? Or did they imagine they no longer needed His assistance?

Franklin's Wise Words

"Franklin went on to say: 'I have lived, Sir, a long time and the longer I live, the more convincing proofs I see of this truth.... that God governs in the affairs of men. And if a sparrow cannot fall to the ground without His notice, is it probable that an empire can rise without His aid? We have been assured, Sir, in the Sacred Writings, that 'except the Lord build the house, they labor in vain that built it.' I firmly believe this, and I also believe that without His concurring aid, we shall succeed in this political building no better, than the builders of Babel: We shall be divided by our little partial local interests; our projects will be confounded; and we ourselves shall become a reproach and bye word down to further ages. And what is worse, mankind may hereafter from the unfortunate instance, despair of establishing governments by human wisdom and leave it to chance, war and conquest.

'I therefore beg leave to move.... that henceforth prayers, imploring the assistance of Heaven and its blessings on our deliberations, be held in the Assembly every morning before we proceed to business, and that one or more of the clergy of this city be requested to officiate in that service.'[3]

"Benjamin Franklin's request to have clergy at the Assembly was not passed because they did not have funds to pay for a full time pastor. However, Mr. Edmund Randolph proposed that they seek volunteer clergy to preach and lead congress in prayer. The system worked well, and after their three-day break, they started the next session in prayer. This was a turning point in debate, and all the delegates showed more respect for each other. Soon, the Connecticut Compromise was introduced and passed, allowing for the Senate to have equal representation from each state and the U.S. House of Representatives to be represented according to each state's size. The convention came together to solve the problem and everyone was satisfied.[4]

"Aidan and Finn, that's why all states have two representatives in the U.S. Senate but the population of a state determines their number of representatives in the House of Representatives.

Prayer Continues to be Important

"In the founding era, prayer was answered and continued to be an important part of our system of government. One of President Washington's first acts as President of the United States was to recommend that there be a permanent chaplain for Congress. He wanted someone who could clarify the Scriptures and remind the legislators to humbly seek God's direction. What a glorious start for a new nation!" Mom concluded.

"Wow, that was amazing," said Aidan. "Just think, our Founding Fathers really did rely on prayer. Come on, Finn, I think we can work this out. How about if you get to stand closer to the pitcher? It will be fun to have a game just for the two of us."

"Cool!" replied Finn, with a big grin on his face. "Thanks for looking out for the little guy." With that, the boys began tossing their baseballs back and forth in their gloves and headed for the door.

Note: At the time of the Constitutional Convention there was no money available to pay chaplains on a full-time basis.

Local chaplains were contacted and volunteered their time to lead the delegates in prayer. One of the first acts of the newly-formed Congress of the United States was to provide chaplains to open the sessions of Congress and the Supreme Court in prayer which is still done today.

[1] Dr. Peter A. Lillback, *Freedom's Holy Light*. Providence Forum. 2000, p 11
[2] Lillback, Dr. Peter A. *Freedom's Holy Light*. Providence Forum. 2000, P 11
[3] Mark Beliles and Stephen McDowell, *America's Providential History*, p 171-172
[4] Mark Beliles and Stephen McDowell, *America's Providential History*, p 172-173

The Constitutional Convention

Of the 55 representatives who participated in the Constitutional Convention, all but three were members of an orthodox Christian church: approximately 29 Anglicans, 16-18 Calvinists, two Methodists, two Lutherans, two Roman Catholics, one lapsed Quaker, and one open Deist.[1]

Benjamin Franklin was the one who listed himself as a deist. There are many questions concerning Franklin's religious beliefs because he attended every kind of Christian worship, called for public prayer, and contributed to all denominations. He always supported public involvement in Christianity. One possible reason he called himself a deist could be a difference in definition. In the past, some considered a deist one who did not designate a particular denomination.

We will never know for sure, but by reading his writings, we can be very confident that, at the very least, he had a Christian worldview.

[1] M.E. Bradford, A Worthy Company, sited in Tim LaHaye's *Faith of our Founding Fathers*, p 30

Our Constitutional Republic

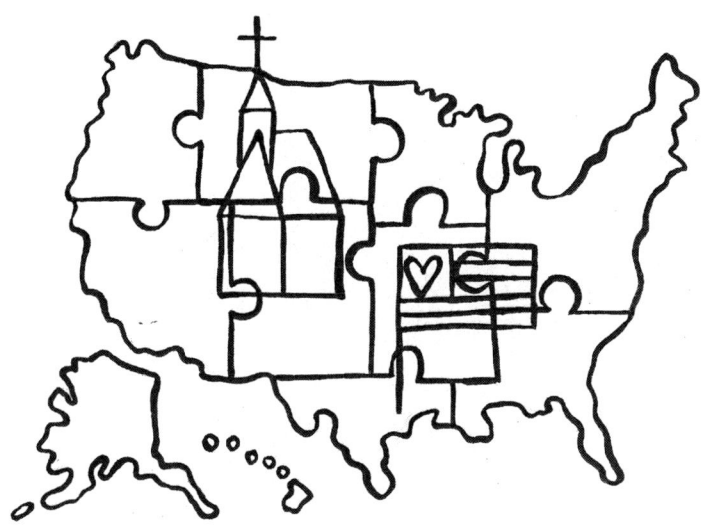

"... And the first place winner in the children's division is the entry, **We Are America**. Will the children of the *We Are America* float please come forward to accept your award!" exclaimed the announcer.

Freja, Isla and their six cousins marched proudly to the front where the announcer stood to accept their recycled trophy. They were thrilled! They had worked so hard on their float and now, for the second year in a row, they had won a trophy in the Madeline Island Fourth of July parade. It was a red, white and blue day!

The cousins passed the trophy around, smiled broadly and thanked everyone as they returned to their spot on the lawn in front of the historical museum. As the program continued, they cheered for other float winners, sang patriotic songs and listened to several speeches about America. One very distinguished older man in an Army uniform talked about how the military fought to achieve and preserve our democracy.

Another spoke of our republic. When the ceremony was over, the two girls headed toward the park for the annual picnic and fundraiser.

Democracy and Republic – What's the Difference?

Ilsa was deep in thought as she walked along. "I don't understand. Do the words democracy and republic mean the same thing? "

Freja quickly answered, "Well, I think there is a difference, but people use both words and think they mean the same thing."

They turned a corner and noticed that the old historical schoolhouse had a big sign welcoming people to tour the building.

Freja said, "Oh, let's go in and look around. We have time because it will take a while for the others to get to the park for the hot dog feed."

With that, they headed into the restored school house. It was complete with rustic wooden desks and an old pot-bellied stove used to warm the building on cold wintry days. Chalkboards were on the walls and there were oil lamps on the table, and only a couple of electric lights hanging from the ceiling. There were no computers, televisions or CD players to be seen. A nice volunteer lady dressed in an early 20th century costume stood behind a wooden desk and welcomed them with a big smile.

The girls noticed a large plaque with the Pledge of Allegiance printed on it. Ilsa walked to the wall and started to read out aloud. "I pledge allegiance to the flag of the United States of America, and to the republic for which it stands, one nation indivisible with liberty and justice for all." Ilsa stopped and asked, "Why doesn't it say 'under God'?"

"Oh, that's easy," said Freja. "They did not add under God until after this school was closed. I think Congress voted to change the pledge and add the words 'under God' when President Eisenhower was in office."

In God We Trust

"That's right," said the volunteer as she moved closer to the girls. "I'm Mrs. Danielson, and I can answer any questions you might have about what you see here. Our country has a long and strong heritage of honoring God and so the words, *under God*, were added to the pledge on Flag Day in 1954. The term, *In God we Trust*, became our official national motto in 1956 after being used unofficially since the founding of our country. It is in the last stanza of our national anthem: 'This be our motto, in God is our trust.' Abraham Lincoln also used the term in the Gettysburg Address in 1863."

Ilsa thought for a moment and then said, "I have another question. Why does it say we pledge allegiance to the United States of America and to the republic? What does republic mean? "

"That's a very good question," replied Mrs. Danielson, cheerfully. Then she explained, "Our form of government is a republic, meaning we elect representatives to cast votes on our behalf."

"I know we are a republic because I learned that in school," said Freja, "but aren't we also a democracy? After all, we have freedom and liberty -- and isn't that really a democracy?"

True Meaning of Democracy

"Not exactly. The true meaning of democracy is a combination of two Greek words – demos (the people) and kratia (the government). In a true democracy, it literally means that every eligible voter would have to vote on every law being considered by the government. Our Founding Fathers understood that kind of system would not be workable for our large country. It could easily lead to mob rule as people would tend to vote only for their own interests and not the interests of the country,"[1] explained Mrs. Danielson.

She continued, "In the United States, all eligible voters are given the right to vote for their own representatives -- making our form of government a republic. Some call it a *democratic republic* because the people vote for representatives. A more correct term for our government is *constitutional republic* because we follow a Constitution which was written in 1787 at the Constitutional Convention and ratified by all the 13 original states. Article 4, Section 4 of our United States Constitution states the following: 'The United States shall guarantee to every State in the Union a Republican Form of Government, and shall protect each of them against Invasions: and against domestic Violence.' "

"Our Founding Fathers provided us with a representative form of government with limits on the elected officials and our government so that our government could never become a monarchy or result in tyranny. Because we have a Constitution, we cannot be called a pure democracy," said Mrs. Danielson, with both great pride and pleasure.

"I never knew I could learn so much in an old schoolhouse that doesn't even have a computer!" said Ilsa. "We do need to get going, but thanks for all your information. I love this island."

"Let's go," Freja said as she grabbed Ilsa's hand and headed out the door. "We'll send our cousins over after lunch; they need to see this, too. Thanks again."

[1] W. Cleon Skousen, *The Making of America*, p 264

The Federalist Papers

After the writing of the Constitution at the Constitutional Convention, James Madison, Alexander Hamilton and John Jay wrote the Federalist Papers. These writings explained to everyone the intent of the convention delegates in establishing the document creating a new government. The Federalist Papers helped convince the people to ratify the Constitution.

In these important historical documents, James Madison defined the words "democracy" and "republic" according to the general thinking of the Convention.

Pure Democracy

Democracies have ever been spectacles of turbulence and contention; have ever been found incompatible with personal security or the rights of property; and have in general been as short in their lives as they have been violent in their deaths.

Federalist Papers No. 10, page 81

In a democracy, the people meet and exercise the government in person; in a republic they assemble and administer it by their representatives and agents.

Federalist Papers No. 14, page 100

Republic

We may define a republic to be… a government which derives all its powers directly or indirectly from the great body of the people, and is administered by people holding their office during (the people's) pleasure for a limited time period or during good behavior.

Federalist Papers No. 39, page 241

Part III

Spotlight: Influential Founding Fathers

George Washington: The Preacher of Providence

Memory Verse:
- Psalm 16:1 – *"Keep me safe, O God, for in you I take refuge."*

It is 1853 and Betsy, a young woman and a descendent of slaves that worked at Mount Vernon (George Washington's home), is helping to restore the plantation for the public to enjoy. Listen in as she shares her story with workers who have come to help in the restoration.

Welcome to Mount Vernon, and I thank you for coming. Soon, we will get this beautiful estate ready as a historic residence. It has been unused for many years, and it needs repair and painting. Many boys and girls and their families will wish to visit this historic place. This is the home of the father of our country, President George Washington and his wonderful wife, Martha.

We all love telling stories of Master Washington and the Mistress. They were God-fearing people and kind to everyone. My family, years and years ago, worked on this estate as slaves. At the time of Master Washington's death, he freed his slaves because he always wished to rid our country of slavery. My family now lives here in Alexandria, just down the road, along the Mount Vernon Parkway.

I would like you to hear some of the stories about the President. I think you will be quite amazed.

The Cherry Tree

My favorite is the story of George Washington and the cherry tree. When he was a young boy, his father gave him a fancy knife for his birthday. Well, he wanted to see just how sharp it was and so he went down by the river and cut down a small cherry tree. The tree didn't have a big trunk, but it was one that his mother prized. When his father saw the tree chopped down, he immediately suspected George and asked him, "Did you chop down the cherry tree?"

George took a deep breath and said, "Oh, Sir, I cannot tell a lie. I did it. I chopped down the cherry tree." Well, we never did hear of his punishment -- or even if the story was really true. But I can tell you that he was always known for telling the truth, and everyone respected him for it.

Rules of Civility and Decent Behavior

Now, Master Washington was a very able young man and his mama taught him from the Bible and made sure he would bring honor to God. He was the oldest of six children. At age 11, his father died and he was never able to go to school or have a formal education. When he was just 15, he read the *110 Rules of Civility and Decent Behavior in Company and Conversation* and was quite taken by what he read.[1] In fact, he copied them in his own handwriting and memorized them.

Let me tell you some of my favorites; I have found them to be very helpful.

Number	Rule
5	If you cough, sneeze, sigh or yawn, do it not loud but privately, and speak not in your yawning, but put your handkerchief or hand before your face and turn aside.
15	Keep your nails clean and short, also your hands and teeth clean, yet without showing any great concern for them.
22	Show not yourself glad at the misfortune of another though he were your enemy.
108	When you speak of God, or His attributes, let it be serious and with reverence.
109	Let your recreations be manful, not sinful.

Now back to stories of Master Washington.

God's Protection

He loved his Bible and had great faith in **the providence of God**, or in other words, that God had control in the affairs of man. One time when he was a young man, Mr. Washington was a soldier, a junior officer, in a British Brigade. This was long before the American Revolution and he had joined the brigade to fight the French and the Indians. On this occasion, the Indians and the French set an ambush for the British brigade. They surprised them and it was a terrible battle. The British were no match for the Indians and French, so the British soldiers were falling all around Washington. And yet Washington was never wounded, even though two horses were shot out from under him.

When the battle was over, Washington took off his topcoat and discovered four bullet holes in his coat. Any of these bullets could have killed him, yet his skin was unbroken. Most of the other officers in his brigade had been killed. He wrote home, "But, by the all-powerful dispensations of providence (God), I have been protected beyond all human probability or expectation..."[2]

Years later, he traveled to the same territory and an Indian, now an old man, came out to meet him. He said that he was at that battle and had told his braves to bring down the tall man on horseback. Everyone aimed at him, but he would not fall. The Indian said he finally decided that he was seeing one who was protected by the spirits, and he told his braves to not shoot any more. The Indian Chief wanted to meet this man that he knew God had saved for something big.[3]

At War with England

After the Declaration of Independence was signed, we were officially at war with England. The English had a very experienced army with many well trained men. The colonies did not have any army, or even any kind of organized group. They only had what were called the minutemen. These were men from individual churches; each of these men owned a gun and was willing to fight for the freedom of their new country at a moment's notice. When they looked for a leader, they chose George Washington to become the Commander of the Continental Army. He was very young to be a general and probably should not have been selected, but he felt it was part of God's plan.

Washington once called himself the "Preacher of Providence," because he worked with the soldiers during the

Revolutionary War. He set rules and guidelines for his new army and asked each soldier to begin each day in prayer led by an officer.

Here were Washington's rules for soldiers under his command during Revolutionary War:

- All profanity was banned.
- All conduct that might offend a citizen whose support they depended upon was banned.
- There would be direct punishment to anyone who offended God or man.
- He also gave a circular order that the colonels or commanding officers of each regiment were directed to procure Chaplains, who were like ministers.[4]

Now, the story of the Revolutionary War is long and I do not have time to tell you all the stories of Mr.—I mean General—Washington, but I know that God had his hand on the outcome many times. General Washington would tell the household about impossible situations, and yet the outcome would be in his favor. He likened it to the Bible where God affected many battles to protect the Israelites.

Like Jehoshaphat's Army

2 Chronicles 20 has a story very similar to what happened to the small, ill-equipped army under the command of General Washington. King Jehoshaphat of Judah was warned that a great army was coming to destroy their nation. A prophet told the king to not be afraid, because the battle was not his, but God's. Sure enough, amazing things happened while the small army of Judah prayed and sang praises to the Lord. Ambushes were set for the invading army and in the end, the enemy turned on themselves and gave victory to Judah. Jehoshaphat and the people's prayers were answered.

Kneeling at Valley Forge

There is a wonderful picture of George Washington kneeling in prayer by his horse on a cold evening during his stay at Valley Forge. It depicts a scene that was witnessed by a Quaker man as he passed through the woods. A relative of Mr. Isaac Potts, a woman named Ruth Ann Potts, relayed this story.

"In 1777, while the American army lay at Valley Forge, a good old Quaker by the name of Isaac Pots had occasion to pass through a thick woods near headquarters. As he traversed the dark brown forest, he heard, at some distance in front of him, a voice which, as he advanced, sounded more fervent and impassioned.

Approaching with slowness and circumspection, whom should he behold in a dark bower, apparently formed for such purpose, but the Commander-in Chief of the armies of the United Colonies – George Washington -- on his knees in the act of devotion to the Ruler of the Universe. At the very moment when his friend Potts, concealed by the trees, approached, he overheard Washington as he was interceding for his beloved country.

With tones of gratitude that, labored for adequate obscurity, had exalted him to the head of a great nation, and that nation fighting at fearful odds for all the world hold dear ...

As soon as the General had finished his devotions and had retired, his friend Potts returned to his house and threw himself into a chair next to his wife. "Heigh! Isaac" said she with tenderness," thee seems agitated. What's the matter?"

"Indeed, my dear," quoth he, "if I appear agitated 'tis no more than what I am. I have seen this day what I shall never forget. 'Til now I have thought that a Christian and a soldier were characters incompatible: but if George Washington be not a man of God, I am mistaken, and still more shall I be disappointed if God does not, through him, perform some great thing for the country. "[5]

> **What about you?**
>
> George Washington prayed for our country. Do you pray for our country? The Bible commands us to do just that. Will you remember to pray for our country and our current president tonight during your prayers? (See Daniel 9 and 1 Timothy 2).

Victory for the United States

General Washington and the continental army won victory for the United States—yes, that was the new name of our colonies. He was selected President of the Constitutional Convention that gathered and wrote the Constitution for this new nation. Again, there was much debate and discussion, but there was a strong desire by most of those present to seek God's guidance for this new government.

In 1789, George Washington was elected the first President of the United States. He was so humble and so in awe over this position as President that at his inauguration, he asked to have a Bible brought forth and had it opened to Genesis 49-50. He took the oath with his left hand on the Bible and his right hand held up.[6]

George Washington was considered the most popular man in the colonies and was described by Henry Lee, a representative to the Constitutional Convention, in his famous tribute of Washington: "First in war, first in peace, and first in the hearts of the countrymen."[6] He was so popular that he could have been crowned king! In fact, some people wanted him to be king. He knew the United States Constitution was better than a monarchy, and so he quietly left office after his second term.

He died in 1799 and is buried on the grounds of Mount Vernon next to his wife, Martha.

Soon everyone will be able to visit Mount Vernon and learn the history of the Preacher of Providence.

[1] Catherine Millard, *Great American Statesmen and Heroes*, p 79-80
[2] David Barton, *The Bulletproof George Washington*, p 47
[3] David Barton, *The Bulletproof George Washington*, p 50-51
[4] Peter Marshall and David Manuel, *The Light and the Glory*, p 289-290
[5] Catherine Millard, *Great American Statesmen and Heroes*, p 79-80
[6] William Federer, *America's God and Country*, p 635

Hello

In his inaugural address in 1789, George Washington said, *"It would be peculiarly improper to omit, in this official act, my fervent supplications to the Almighty Being who rules over the universe and who presides in the councils of nations..."*

Farewell

In his farewell address in 1796, George Washington said, *"Of all the dispositions and habits which lead to political prosperity, religion and morality are indispensable supports. In vain would that man claim the tribute of patriotism, who should labor to subvert these great pillars of human happiness, these firmest props of the duties of men and citizens."*

1740-1760: The Great Awakening
Jonathan Edwards & George Whitefield

The Great Awakening was actually a re-awakening of the need to return to the covenant way of life, or in other words, the need to follow Scripture. Prosperity and a gradual turning from God had caused a spiritual malaise. The religious zeal of the Pilgrims and Puritans was in a spiritual slumber.

One of the best known of the preachers during this time was Jonathan Edwards. He preached against allowing the new thinking to swallow up Christianity, and he brought thousands back to Christ. His most revered sermon was *Sinners in the Hands of an Angry God* and copies of it were circulated throughout the colonies, forcing many to face their sinful nature and return to repentance and to God.

George Whitefield was an Anglican preacher from England and known as a great orator. He was the first to take to the streets and fields and gather huge crowds to listen to his sermons. It is said that he had such a loud voice that he could speak to thousands at a time without any amplification. He prepared and gave over a hundred sermons a month and traveled constantly. Because he was friends with Benjamin Franklin, he had access to funds to build a large stadium at the University of Pennsylvania so he could preach to large crowds.

The Great Awakening brought many changes to the colonies and a new way of communicating among colonies. It did the following which were very important to future events:

- Awakened a new spirituality based on following Jesus Christ.
- For the first time, large groups of people gathered together. The importance of geographic borders of the colonies was diminished.
- Brought Christians together from all denominations.
- Raised up the voices of the Christian clergy.

"Without the Great Awakening (1740-1760), there would have been no American Revolution (1760-1790). The ideas, the motivation, the Biblical worldview, and the great virtuous statesmanship seen in the founder's era were all birthed in the great revival led by Jonathan Edwards and George Whitefield."[1]

[1] Mark Beliles and Stephen McDowell, *America's Providential History*, p 127

The Importance of the Christian Religion

Noah Webster spent 26 years writing the first American Dictionary of the English language. It contained 70,000 entries and 12,000 new definitions and was published in 1828. It standardized spelling and made communication more exact.

In the preface of this work, he wrote:

"In my view, the Christian religion is the most important and one of the first things in which all children under a free government ought to be instructed. No truth is more evident to my mind that the Christian religion must be the basis of any government intended to secure the rights and privileges of a free people."

William Federer, *American's God and Country*, p 677

Noah Webster
"Education Without the Bible is Useless."

The Founding Fathers firmly believed in education, and the main goal of education was primarily to be able to read the Scriptures. The first common school was Boston Lake School, founded in 1636, for children who did not have a parent to teach them.

In 1647, the legislature of Massachusetts enacted the "Old Deluder Satan" law. Its purpose was to stop Satan from keeping men from the knowledge of the Scriptures. This law required every township with 50 families or more to provide a school for their children so they could learn to read God's word. Colleges were founded by Christian denominations.

Higher Education in Colonial America[1]

Date	College	Colony	Affiliation
1636	Harvard	Massachusetts	Puritan
1693	William and Mary	Virginia	Anglican
1701	Yale	Connecticut	Congregational
1746	Princeton	New Jersey	Presbyterian
1754	Columbia	New York	Anglican
1764	Brown	Rhode Island	Baptist
1766	Rutgers	New Jersey	Dutch Reform
1769	Dartmouth	New Hampshire	Congregational

The first text book printed in America (in 1777) was *The New England Primer*, a small book for young children that used Scripture and Christian principles to teach reading and the Biblical worldview. The Bible and Watts Hymnal were also widely used.

DeMar, Gary, *America's Heritage,* p 42

His Justice Cannot Sleep Forever

"God who gave us life, gave us liberty. And can the liberties of a nation be thought secure when we have removed their only firm basis, a conviction in the minds of the people that these liberties are the gift of God? That they are not to be violated but with His wrath?

Indeed, I tremble for my country when I reflect that God is just; that His justice cannot sleep forever."

Thomas Jefferson
From his notes on the state of Virginia, 1781

Judgment of Heaven

George Mason was a devout Christian from Virginia, and although he was a slaveholder, he wanted to stop slavery.

During the Constitutional Convention, he said, *"Every master of slaves is born a petty tyrant. They bring the judgment of heaven upon a country.* **As nations cannot be rewarded or punished in the next world, they must be in this. By an inevitable chain of causes and effects, Providence punishes national sins by national calamities."**

Mark Beliles and Stephen McDowell,, *America's Providential History*, p 227

Signers of the Constitution
All Men are Created Equal

The signers of the Constitution faced a big dilemma regarding how to deal with slavery. Slavery has been around since right after the Fall, when Adam and Eve sinned. Slavery started when one group of people conquered another, and the conquered group became their servants or slaves. Slavery is part of the sinful nature of man.

When the Pilgrims and Puritans came to the New World, they knew all about slavery and servanthood. In fact, in the early days of this country, many people, both black and white, came to this country as indentured servants. Someone else paid their passage to the New World, and he/she owed money or work to the financial provider. Often, they worked up to seven years to pay back the money for their voyage, but after the seven years, the servant was free.

During early colonial days, many black colonists were free men who owned land and held a variety of jobs. Several were elected to government jobs and held positions of great honor. During the Revolutionary War, black soldiers fought side by side with white soldiers. When George Washington crossed the Delaware, there were two black soldiers with him in the boat.

African Slaves

About the same time the Pilgrims came to America, slave traders found a new way of making a large amount of money at the expense of men, women and children from Africa. Fellow Africans trapped and held natives and sold them to trade merchants, who then transported them around the world to be sold into slave labor. The first such ship landed in Virginia in 1619. However, the Puritans were so outraged when one such ship docked in Massachusetts that they arrested the captain and returned the captured people to their homeland.[1]

Almost all the Founding Fathers rejected slavery and saw it as a sin against not only man, but God. In fact, many of the colonies wrote in their constitutions that slavery was expressly forbidden. The colonies petitioned King George III to prevent the importation of slaves, but he vetoed all colonial laws abolishing slavery or ending the slave trade.[2]

George Washington

In 1786, late in George Washington's career, he said," It is among my first wishes to see some plan adopted by which slavery in this country shall be abolished by law." The slaves of both George Washington and Thomas Jefferson were to be freed according to their last will and testament. Benjamin Rush, a signer of the Declaration of Independence, and Benjamin Franklin were two of many Founding Fathers who started abolition societies to eliminate slavery from the United States.

When it came time to write the Constitution, there was debate as to whether to outlaw slavery immediately or let it die out naturally. Some spoke eloquently to ban it, but others were determined to retain slavery and pointedly said if slavery were banned, they would not join the union. Many plantation owners had borrowed vast sums of money to purchase slaves. If slavery was immediately abolished, many felt the economy of the south would collapse and that it would put the new country into an economic depression.

So the writers faced a big dilemma. They desperately wanted a union of all 13 colonies and they were aware of great movements for ending the practice of slavery. Many of the northern states banned slavery in their constitutions and the Northwest Ordinance prohibited any new state to own slaves. There was loud vocal opposition to the institution of slavery, especially by the clergy who continually spoke against it. Both England and United States enacted legislation to stop the importing of slaves, but sadly, slavery continued.

The United States Constitution

The Constitution did not endorse slavery, but it did address it. The Constitution did not completely abolish slavery, but it did make two major steps forward:

1. "The southern states agreed to acknowledge that blacks were persons in the eyes of the law for the first time. Although they only were counted as 3/5's of a person, it was a major concession nonetheless." [3] Abolitionists, those working to stop slavery, did not want to count slaves because representation was determined by population. If each slave had been counted the number of representatives from the slave states would have been greater giving pro-slavery legislators more votes in congress. (Article 1, Section 2)

2. Article 1 Section 9 of the Constitution allowed for the importation of slaves only until 1808 (20 years into the future).[3] At that time, Congress did what the Founding Fathers had wanted to do and stopped the importing of slaves. This sunset clause which ended importing of slaves was a big concession by the delegates from southern states. Note that the Founding Fathers were ahead of their time. English legislator, William Wilberforce, did not convince England to stop importing slaves until 1807, only one year before it was stopped in America and 19 years after the Founding Fathers wrote it into the United States Constitution. Needless to say, the hope that stopping slave trade would end slavery did not occur for either England or the United States.

3. There is a third mention of those in servitude in the Constitution (Article 4, Section 2) which allowed slave owners to reclaim any runaway slave from another state. Not until 1850 did this become a widely used, dangerous, unjust law when new pro-slavery legislators enacted the Fugitive Slave Act of 1850 giving power to unscrupulous bounty hunters and immoral owners.

The Northwest Ordinance

Another document, the Northwest Ordinance, prevented new territories from becoming a state if they allowed slavery. This was changed in 1820, after the founding era, by the passing of the Missouri Compromise, which was in direct conflict with the ideals and values of the Founding Fathers. It allowed slavery in almost half of the existing territories.

By 1810, some people began justifying slavery and considered it an important economic institution. After all, slavery provided labor to pick cotton for the newly invented cotton gin and to harvest the ever popular tobacco.

The Position of the Church

Many clergy rejected the new thinking and worked to eliminate slavery by preaching against it, forming abolition societies and offering direct help to slaves.[4] Abolition Societies started even before the Revolutionary War. One third of the abolitionist leaders were clergy who worked tirelessly to provide an underground railroad as well as elect anti-slavery leaders.

The sins of the nation ended in a Civil War, which caused death and heartache.

[1] David Barton, *Setting the Record Straight: American History in Black and White*, p 6
[2] John Chalfant, *America – A Call to Greatness*, p 50
[3] Mark Beliles and Stephen McDowell, *America's Providential History*, p 226-227
[4] David Barton, *Setting the Record Straight: American History in Black and White*, p 18-30

Part IV

Foundational Symbols & Documents

1620:
The Mayflower Compact

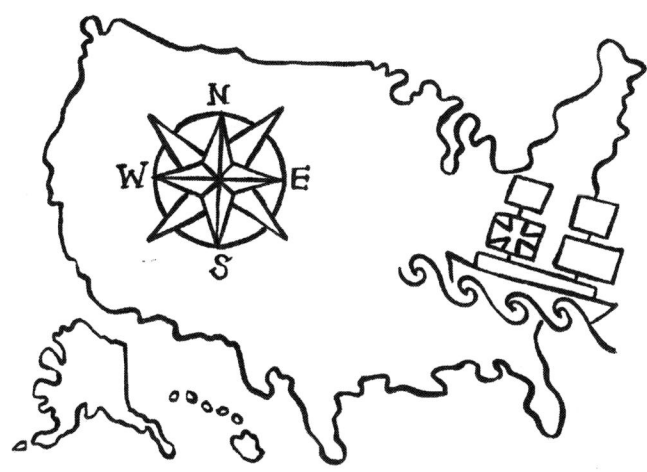

Just the Facts
- *Place:* Plymouth, Massachusetts
- *Date:* 1620
- *Purpose:* To draft a governing document and choose the leaders to rule the new community in the same way that Pilgrims choose their church leaders.
- *Method:* 42 men, representing each household, voted so that the government reflected the common good and consent of all those governed. Each person wrote down their ideas and then discussed them and reached consensus on the rules that should govern their society. This Compact remained in effect until 1691 when Plymouth was absorbed into the Massachusetts Bay Colony.

How It All Began
See the background information on page 33 of this booklet.

Text from the Mayflower Compact
(emphasis added)

In the name of God, Amen. We whose names are under-written, the loyal subjects of our dread Sovereign Lord, King James, by the Grace of God, of Great Britain, France, Ireland, King, Defender of the Faith, etc.

Having undertaken, **for the glory of God and advancement of the Christian faith** *and honor of our King and country, a voyage to plant the first colony in the northern parts of Virginia, do by these presents solemnly and mutually in the presence of God and one of another, covenant and combine ourselves together into a civil body politic, for our better ordering and preservation and furtherance of the ends aforesaid, and by virtue hereof to enact, constitute and frame such just and equal laws, ordinances, acts, Constitutions and offices from time to time, as shall be thought most meet and convenient for the general good of the colony.*

Unto which we promise all due submission and obedience, in witness whereof we have hereunder subscribed our names at Cape Cod, the 11 of November, in the year of the reign of our Sovereign King James of England...

Anno Domini 1620

1751: The Liberty Bell

Memory Verse
- Leviticus 25:10 - *Proclaim liberty throughout all the land unto all the inhabitants thereof."*

Just the Facts
- *Place:* Philadelphia
- *Date:* 1751
- *Why:* To celebrate the 50th anniversary of William Penn's Charter of Privileges

How It All Began

In 1751, a large bell was ordered from the White Chapel Foundry in England to be placed in the newly-constructed State House in Pennsylvania. The bell was used to celebrate the 50th anniversary of Quaker William Penn's Charter of Privileges. This charter governed the people of Penn's Colony and granted those living in the colony of Pennsylvania the freedom to worship according to their own desires without condemnation. Isaac Norris, a Quaker, selected the Leviticus 25:10 verse to be inscribed on the bell. The verse commemorates the 50 year Jubilee Celebration by the Hebrew nation.

The bell was hung in the steeple of Independence Hall and was rung to announce events and celebrations within Pennsylvania and later the United States. It rang loud and clear on the first 4th of July (Independence Day).

On July 4, 1826, exactly 50 years after Congress voted to accept the Declaration of Independence, both Thomas Jefferson and John Adams died. The liberty bell rang in tribute to the two Founding Fathers.

Think about it...

Isn't that amazing that both men who were so responsible for the Declaration of Independence would die on the same day, exactly 50 years after the signing of the Declaration? Do you think the Providence of God had something to do with the coincidence of their deaths on that particular day? Remember providence means the intervention of God in man's affairs.

In 1836, while tolling the death of Chief Justice John Marshall, the liberty bell cracked and that put an end to its part in the founding period. The crack was small at first, but continued to grow. Today, the crack splits the word "liberty."

Through the years, the bell was known by many different names and did not become known as the Liberty Bell until 1839. It was the abolitionists, those who opposed slavery, who named it and used it as a symbol to represent freedom.[1]

In 1873, the Liberty Bell was lowered to a spot directly below the tower of Independence Hall and additional verses from Leviticus were printed on the support beam.

In January 1976, the old bell was moved from Independence Hall to a modern building near Constitution Hall and will be moved one last time to the slave block display when it is completed. Unfortunately, the support displaying the entire Leviticus verse is no longer on display.[2]

[1] *The Spirit of Liberty Bell*, Providence Forum, www.providenceforum.org
[2] *Rewriting of American History*, Catherine Millard, p 35,

1776:
Declaration of Independence

Just the Facts
- *Place:* Philadelphia
- *Dates:*
  - July 4, 1776 – voted to accept Declaration of Independence
  - August 2, 1776 – members signed Declaration of Independence
- *Purpose:* To establish a new nation
- *Committee selected to write the document:* John Adams, Thomas Jefferson, Roger Sherman, Robert Livingston, Benjamin Franklin
- *Signers:* 56 signed the Declaration

How It All began

The First Continental Congress met in Carpenter Hall in Philadelphia on September 5, 1774. It consisted of representatives from each of the colonies except Georgia. They wanted to determine a strategy for dealing with King George and the growing hostility between the colonies and England. Already the English soldiers were becoming aggressive, and fear was sweeping through the colonies. By 1775, England declared that the colonies were to be put under martial law.

The Second Continental Congress collectively agreed that something had to be done, and the best answer was to separate from England. A committee was asked to write a document stating their decision and listing the reasons. The committee consisted of Benjamin Franklin, John Adams, Roger

Sherman, Robert Livingston and Thomas Jefferson. Jefferson, because of his skill, wrote most of the wording with the others and Congress adding and deleting phrases. He copied word for word some phrases from *The Law of Nature in Government*, a book written in 1717 by John Wise, a pastor.[1]

The ideas in the Declaration were not new, but for the first time, they were combined to establish a new nation. The Declaration brought together the understanding that all people were created equal, were endowed by God, and had unalienable (today, we say inalienable) rights. In other words, rights come from God and not from government or a king. The Declaration stated the new country's reliance upon God three more times.

The Declaration also lists 27 direct grievances that the colonies had against the king and British rule. Contrary to what most say, only one grievance was against unfair taxation. Their main objection was the king's unwillingness to support the laws and legislature of the colonies together with not allowing the colonies to determine their own trade laws. An example was when Virginia enacted a law to stop the importation of slaves and the king abolished the law.

The vote to accept the Declaration of Independence had to be unanimous, without any of the 13 colonies voting against independence. It took several voting times to reach consensus. Delaware had two representatives, one voted for and the other against independence and this caused a real problem. Delaware needed a third representative to break the tie vote, one way or the other. Caesar Rodney had been selected as the third representative, but he was at his farm in Delaware. He was summoned to Congress and rode his horse 89 miles through a terrible storm in order to reach Philadelphia in time to vote. He traveled through a quagmire of mud and often had to dismount and walk to save his horse. He arrived just in time and cast his vote for independence, allowing Delaware to vote for independence. New York abstained from voting, but the vote for independence from Great Britain passed.[2]

The Declaration of Independence proved to be the charter of our nation, or our nation's birth certificate. It established the nation, and the Constitution established the government. The Declaration of Independence made it clear that the United States would operate under the laws of God.[3]

The members of Congress were dedicated and courageous. Just by signing the document they knew they would be hunted down by the British soldiers and considered traitors to the British Empire. They acknowledged this concern at the end of the Declaration of Independence, where they stated, "We pledge to each other our lives, our fortunes and our sacred honor."

[1] Mark Beliles and Stephen McDowell, *America's Providential History*, p 117
[2] Peter Marshall and David Manuel, *The Light and the Glory*, p 306-310
[3] Tim LaHaye, *Faith of our Founding Fathers*, p 38-40

1774: The First Continental Congress

American's first meeting to discuss the future of the New World was called the First Continental Congress. A representative from all but one colony gathered in Carpenter's Hall in Philadelphia on September 5, 1774.

The meeting started with a three-hour prayer by Episcopal clergy, Dr. Jacob Duche'. They asked for God's guidance as they debated separating from England.

Overview of the Declaration of Independence

The Declaration of Independence is divided into four sections, making it easier to read and understand. (The four references to God and the phrase stating "government should get its power from the people" have been reproduced here in bold type for emphasis.)

THE DECLARATION OF INDEPENDENCE
IN CONGRESS, JULY 4, 1776

(A) WHEN in the Course of human events, it becomes necessary for one people to dissolve the political bands which have connected them with another, and to assume among the powers of the earth, the separate and equal station to which the **Laws of Nature and of Nature's God** entitle them, a decent respect to the opinions of mankind requires that they should declare the causes which impel them to the separation.

When the founders wrote of "the Laws of Nature and Nature's God," they understood this to mean what Locke, Blackstone, Montesquieu and others had presented:

- "The Laws of Nature" is the will of God revealed in creation and the conscience of man.

- "The Laws of Nature's God" is the will of God revealed in the Scriptures."[1]

(**B**) WE hold these truths to be self-evident, that all men are created equal, that they are **endowed by their Creator with certain unalienable Rights**, that among these are Life, Liberty, and the pursuit of Happiness. -- That to secure these rights, **Governments are instituted among Men, deriving their just powers from the consent of the governed** -- That whenever any Form of Government becomes destructive of these ends, it is the Right of the People to alter or abolish it, and to institute new Government, laying its foundation on such principles, and organizing its powers in such form, as to them shall seem most likely to affect their Safety and Happiness. Prudence, indeed, will dictate that Governments long established should not be changed for light and transient causes; and accordingly all experience hath shewn, that mankind are more disposed to suffer, while evils are sufferable, than to right themselves by abolishing the forms to which they are accustomed. But when a long train of abuses and usurpations, pursuing invariably the same Object, evinces a design to reduce them under absolute Despotism, it is their right, it is their duty, to throw off such Government, and to provide new Guards for their future security.
-- Such has been the patient sufferance of these Colonies; and such is now the necessity which constrains them to alter their former Systems of Government. The History of the present King of Great Britain is a history of repeated injuries and usurpations, all having in direct object the establishment of an absolute Tyranny over these States. To prove this, let Facts be submitted to a candid world....

The Declaration of Independence says rights are given by God, the Creator and that power comes from the people.

> **(C) Author's note:** *At this point the Declaration contains a list of grievances. Only one addresses the grievance of taxation without representation and it is not the highest ranking. The 26 other grievances were against the British Empire because they would not allow the colonies to set their own laws and direction in agreement with the laws of God.*
>
> **(D)** WE, therefore, the Representatives of the United States of America, in General Congress, Assembled, **appealing to the Supreme Judge of the World** for the rectitude of our intentions, do, in the Name, and by the Authority of the good People of these Colonies, solemnly publish and declare, that these United Colonies are, and of Right ought to be Free and Independent States; that they are Absolved from all Allegiance to the British Crown, and that all political connection between them and the State of Great Britain, is and ought to be totally dissolved; and that as Free and Independent States, they have full Power to levy War, conclude Peace, contract Alliances, establish Commerce, and to do all other Acts and Things which Independent States may of right do. And for the support of this Declaration, with a firm **reliance on the protection of divine Providence,** we mutually pledge to each other our Lives, our Fortunes, and our sacred Honor."

This section stated that they appealed, or asked, the Supreme Judge of the World or God for correctness in their action. They ended by saying that they would rely on the protection of divine Providence, another way of saying God. These two references to God were not included in Jefferson's work but added by the Continental Congress.[1]

[1] Stephen McDowell, *America, A Christian Nation*, p 8

1787:
The United States Constitution

Memory Verse
- Psalm 33:12 - *"Blessed is the nation whose God is the Lord."*

Just the Facts
- *Place:* Philadelphia
- *Date:* 1787
- *Purpose:* To establish a new form of government with a written document.
- *Attendance:* Representatives from all colonies except Rhode Island.
    - 73 representatives were appointed: 55 attended, 39 signed
    - Three refused to sign because of lack of a bill of rights and because of the slavery issue: George Mason, Edmund Randolph, Elbridge Gerry
    - Thomas Jefferson didn't attend; he was in France as U.S. ambassador
- *Important titles:*
    - George Washington - unanimously elected president of the Constitutional Convention
    - James Madison - often called the Father of the U.S. Constitution

How It Began

After the signing of the Declaration of Independence in 1776, the Continental Congress established a method of working together under the Articles of Confederation. This system allowed the colonies to work as a committee of states during the Revolutionary War but granted little, if any, power to a federal government because the colonists were afraid of trading King George for a local monarch.

When independence was won, the Articles were ineffective. They had no executive (president) or person in charge, no judiciary, no power to tax or to enforce the law.

In 1787, the Constitutional Convention was called to session to examine and possibly change the Articles of Confederation. However, it soon became clear that it was impossible, so they began the arduous task of writing a new Constitution to establish a new government ruled by the people rather than kings or the elite.

The representatives all had a broad knowledge of history, philosophy and the Bible. Dr. Francis Schaffer, an influential Christian philosopher of the 20th century, said that the founders had what could be a "Christian consensus" or a Christian worldview.

They believed:

- Unalienable rights are from God and not government.
  - **The rights to life, liberty and property come from God, not government.**

- Man is sinful and human nature is self-serving and needs boundaries.
  - **Separation of powers – no branch could become all powerful**
  - **Checks and balances**
  - **Limited government**

- Government should serve the people and not the other way around.
  - **"Government is of the people, by the people, and for the people."** John Wycliffe, 1385, quoted by Abraham Lincoln in the Gettysburg Address.

- Moral, religious and educated people are necessary for good government.
    - **George Washington said, "Of all the dispositions and habits which lead to political prosperity, religion and morality are indispensible supports."**
    - **Congress** declared in the Northwest Ordinance of 1787...**Religion and morality and knowledge, being necessary to good government and the happiness of mankind, schools and the means of education shall forever be encouraged.**

- A central government that is too strong can lead to tyranny. A central government too weak can lead to chaos.

A Religious and Moral People

On April 17, 1787, Benjamin Franklin said, "Only virtuous people are capable of freedom. As nations become corrupt and vicious, they have more need of masters."

On October 11, 1798, then President John Adams said, "We have no government armed with power capable of contending with human passions unbridled by morality and religion. Avarice, ambition, revenge and gallantry would break the strongest cords of our Constitution as a whale goes through a net. Our Constitution was made only for a moral and religious people. It is wholly inadequate to the government of any other.

God's Law Provides for Liberty

Constitution	Concept	Scripture
Article 1, Section 8 To establish Uniform Rules of Naturalization	Immigration should be fair and equitable.	Leviticus 19:34 - **You shall treat the stranger who sojourns with you as the native among you.**
Article 2, Section 1 No person except a Natural born Citizen.. shall be eligible to the Office of President	The president shall have loyalty to this nation and government.	Deuteronomy 17:15 - **One from among your brothers you shall set as a king over you. You may not put a foreigner over you who is not your brother.**
Article 4, Section 4 The United States shall guarantee to every state in the Union a Republican Form of Government.	Federalism separates power between local, county, state and federal, each with their own authority thus providing division of power.	Exodus 18: 21 - **Look for able men who fear God, who are trustworthy, and hate a bribe, and place such men over the people as chiefs of thousands, of hundreds, of fifties and tens.**
Article 1, Section 8 To fix the Standards of weights and measures	This provides for fair transactions in commerce.	Deuteronomy 25 – **You do not have two differing weights in your house – one large, one small. You must have accurate and honest weights and measures....**
Three branches of government: Judicial, Executive and Legislative	This provides for the separation of powers and checks and balances.	Isaiah 33:22 - **For the Lord is our "judge", the Lord is our "lawgiver", the Lord is our "king."**

The United States Constitution

Constitution	Concept	Scripture
The Constitution protects unalienable (God given) rights.	These rights of life, liberty and property shall not be taken away by government.	Daniel 4:17 - **"God made the world and everything in it."** Romans 13:1 – **The authorities that exist have been established by God.**
Provides equality for all under the law.	They knew that the majority should never trample the minority, nor should the minority trample the majority.	Job 34:19 – **"He is not partial to princes, nor does he regard the rich more than the poor; for they are all the work of His hands."**
Article 1, Section 7 If any bill shall not be returned by the president within 10 days (Sunday exception) it shall be law.	Sunday is a day revered by the Christian faith.	Deuteronomy 5:12 – **"Observe the Sabbath day and keep it holy."**
Constitution Closes… In the year of our Lord one thousand seven hundred and eighty-seven	Uses the Julian calendar which honors the birth of Christ	

The Constitution has often been called a miracle document: no such constitution had ever been written or used to form a government before 1787. It has endured for over 230 years. The French have had seven different constitutions since their revolution which occurred soon after the American Revolution. Italy is now on its 51st.

The Constitution is considered "enduring" because it was written to provide a firm framework that can only be changed by states passing an amendment or by holding a constitutional convention. A constitutional convention has never been done and is somewhat undefined and therefore carries unknown risks. The Founders purposely made the changing of the Constitution very difficult.

In order to ratify the Constitution it was promised that amendments insuring the rights of the people would be adopted at the first congress. This was done and the first 10 amendments, known as the Bill of Rights , became effective December 15, 1791. Only 27 amendments have ever been added to the Constitution.

Quotable Quotes

James Madison, attributed to him in 1778:
"We have staked the whole future of American civilization, not upon the power of government, far from that. We have staked the future of all of our political institutions upon the capacity of mankind for self-government: upon the capacity of each and all of us to govern ourselves to control ourselves according to the Ten Commandments of God."

Abraham Lincoln (16th United States President)
"In regard for this Great Book [the Bible], I have this to say: it is the best gift God has given to man. All the good Savior gave to the world was communicated through this book."

Ronald Reagan (40th United States President)
"Inside the Bible's pages lie all the answers to all the problems man has ever known. ... It is my firm belief that the enduring values present in its pages have a great meaning for each of us and for our nation. The Bible can touch our hearts, order our minds, and refresh our souls."

Quotes from: *The American Patriot's Bible (*New King James Version), Dr. Richard B. Lee, editor

1787:
Preamble to the US Constitution

"We the people" recognizes that the people of the United States have the God-given right to govern themselves. There is no such thing as a divine right of a king or monarch to rule over people as this often leads to tyranny. The rights belong with the citizens and they can exercise that right when they vote for their representatives.

The new Constitution was designed to ensure peace, security and domestic tranquility. The founders recognized that power can corrupt even the best of men and that there is a human nature to ever expand one's power. To satisfy the goal of the preamble they wrote the Constitution making people responsible and watchful. This means citizens need to exercise self-government being both respectful and responsible in their own affairs. Possibly this is why so many founders wrote that our form of government was only for a moral and religious people.

> *We the people of the United States, in order to form a more perfect union, establish justice, insure domestic tranquility, provide for the common defense, promote the general welfare, and secure the blessings of liberty to ourselves and our posterity, do ordain and establish this Constitution for the United States of America.*

The Founding Fathers used Christian ideals for their new government. Each concept in the Preamble has a Biblical perspective.

Constitution	Concept	Scripture
To establish justice	Government role	1 Peter 2:14 "....to punish those who do wrong and to commend those who do right."
To insure domestic tranquility	Pray for leaders who are in authority.	(Paul instructs us to pray for leaders) 1 Timothy 2:1- "... that we may live peaceful and quiet lives in all godliness and holiness."
To provide for the common defense	Civil government is to protect and it does not bear the sword for nothing.	Luke 22:36 "... if you don't have a sword, sell your cloak and buy one."
To promote general welfare	Common good needs to be promoted for all and not for individuals and preferred groups.	Proverbs 3:27 ..."Do not withhold good from those to whom it is due."
To secure the blessings of liberty	Blessings are a gift from God, not a privilege granted by government.	2 Corinthians 3:17 - "Now the Lord is the Spirit, and where the Spirit of the Lord is, there is freedom."[1]

[1] Mark Beliles and Stephen McDowell, *America's Providential History*, p 185

Separation of Church and State Is This in The Constitution?

The phrase 'separation of church and state" has been twisted and changed so that today, it literally means, **separation of religious expression from public life**. The phrase "separation of church and state" does not appear in the Declaration of Independence, the United States Constitution or any founding document.

The original source of the phrase has been credited to a letter written by Thomas Jefferson to the Danbury Baptist Church in 1802. In this letter, he assured them the government could not -- and would not -- interfere with their religious freedom or select one denomination to be the state church. Jefferson himself did not separate out the Christian religion from public life. This is shown in just a few of his actions listed below:

- As Governor of Virginia, Jefferson readily issued proclamations for days of public and solemn thanksgiving and prayer to Almighty God.
- As President, he included a prayer in each of his two inaugural addresses.
- In 1803, Jefferson signed an appropriation of funds to be paid to the Catholic Church for the education and religious instruction of the Kaskaskia Indians.
- While president of the United States, he also became the first president of the Washington, D.C. public school board that chose the Bible (the entire Bible) and Watt's Hymnal as reading texts in the classroom.
- As President, he often attended church services in the Capital Building on Sundays.

Our Founders did not want a state controlled church, nor a church controlled state. They had experienced both while in England. The Founders' separation was an institutional separation only; a separation of duties-- but never did they intend a removal of religion from the public arena. We are one nation under God, meaning both state and church have a clear duty, derived from biblical principles.

In a 1957 Supreme Court ruling the court ignored the original intent of the first amendment which states, **"Congress shall make no law respecting an establishment of religion, or prohibiting the free exercise thereof."** The limitation here is clearly on "Congress" not the people. In this precedent-setting decision, they not only ignored the original intent of the constitution but also the original intent of Jefferson's phrase. **They redefined the meaning of the first amendment of the Constitution** and over time, subsequent court cases marginalized religious freedom and eliminated God and Christian symbols from the public sphere.

Excerpts from *Dreamers of a Godless Utopia*, Michael J. Chapman, p 8-9

Let Us Commit our Cause to the Lord

President of the Continental Congress, John Hancock, said as he signed the Declaration of Independence, **"Let us humbly commit our righteous cause to the great Lord of the Universe..."**

Part V

Just For Fun

The Dollar Bill – Share the Facts

Do you want to find a simple way to share the Christian beginnings of our country with family and friends? Dr. Peter Lillback, Providence Forum, uses a common dollar bill.

ON THE FRONT – George Washington
George Washington's face is on the front of the dollar bill. He was our first President and commander of the Continental Army that defeated the English, and he was also one of the spiritual leaders of our country. At one point, he called himself the "Preacher of Providence." (See more information about Washington on page 71 of this booklet.)

ON THE BACK -- In God We Trust
On the back, we find the words "In God We Trust." That phrase was gradually added to currency over many years. It was not until the time of the Civil War that it was added to *all* currency. In fact, the last bill signed by President Abraham Lincoln was to require IN GOD WE TRUST on all currency.

These important words came from the last verse of our National Anthem, which was written by Francis Scott Key during the War of 1812. This song captured the feelings of the people of the new nation, as seen in the last verse of the National Anthem:

O! thus be it ever when free men shall stand
Between their loved home and the war's desolation;
Blest with vict'ry and peace, may the Heav'n-rescued land
Praise the Pow'r that hath made and preserved us a nation!
Then to conquer we must, when our cause it is just;
And this be our motto, "In God is our trust!"
And the star spangled banner in triumph shall wave
O'er the land of the free and the home of the brave!

Next, find two circles on the back of a dollar bill. These are the front and back of the great seal of the United States. Notice the eye above the pyramid and you will see the "Eye of Providence" which identifies God's involvement in the affairs of man and our founding. The pyramid signifies strength and duration. Look at the bottom and you will find Roman numerals reading 1776. Notice the Latin words "annuit coeptis?" It means "He has smiled on our undertakings." When Continental Congress accepted this as the new seal, they very much understood that God had smiled down on them during their fight for a new nation. Many miracles had occurred during those early years.

The Eagle

Look at the other side of the seal and notice the American eagle with a shield. The eagle has become a symbol of the United States. The wide ban on top of the stripes represents the president, or executive branch, which holds all states together. In the shield are 13- stripes representing the 13- original colonies. If you saw this seal in color and not on the dollar bill, the stripes would be red, white, and blue and represent seven moral virtues.

- White for purity and innocence.
- Red for hardiness and valor.
- Blue for vigilance, perseverance and justice.

Under the Shield, you can see the claws holding an olive branch for peace and arrows for defending our country in war.

E Pluribus Unum

The motto E Pluribus Unum means "out of many, one." Immigrants came to America, but they gave up some of their past to work together as one nation. This brought forth the idea that the United States was a melting pot, not a tossed salad.

Novis Ordo Seclorum

Finally, you will find the Latin "Novis Ordo Seclorum" or "a new order of the age." This phrase was used to let everyone know that the new government of the United States was a government that relied on moral virtue and trusted in God and not the old world monarchy.

[1] Peter Lilliback, *The Real Value of the Dollar Bill*, The Providence Forum

---

Test your knowledge of the dollar bill
Quiz on page 114

The Dollar Bill Quiz

- Whose picture is on the dollar bill?

- Was he/she a Christian?

- All currency bears what motto?

- What does the eye on top of the pyramid stand for?

- What does the Latin phrase "e pluribus unum" mean?

- Name the three colors of the seal, if it were printed in color.
  - *Challenge question*: Name the seven virtues that those three colors represent.

- What does the olive branch represent?

- What do the arrows represent?

Well ... how did you do?

If you need to brush up on your facts, go back to page 111 and review the material about the dollar bill.

In God Is Our Trust

Francis Scott Key first coined the phrase when he included it in the Star Spangled Banner's third verse: "In God is our trust." The last official act of President Lincoln was to sign legislation for this motto to be inscribed on all U.S. currency.

On July 3, 1956, President Dwight D. Eisenhower signed a bill making the phrase "In God we trust" the national motto of the United States.

Liberty Bell Quiz

- Where is the bell located?

- When was the Liberty Bell made?

- For what occasion was the Liberty Bell made?

- From what book in the Bible does the inscription come?
  - Extra challenge – What is the inscription?

- When did it crack? What is it best known for?

- Which two Founding Fathers died on the same day, July 4, 1826, exactly 50 years after the ringing of the bell for the voting and acceptance of the Declaration of Independence?

- Who nicknamed it the Liberty Bell?

- Where will the bell eventually be displayed and why?

Well ... how did you do?

If you need to brush up on your facts, go back to page 91 and review the material about the Liberty Bell.

Did You Know?

When the family gathers for dinner, maybe at Thanksgiving, have the guests read the facts concerning our American Christian heritage before giving thanks to God for His many blessings.

- The first Thanksgiving was declared by Governor William Bradford in Plymouth, Massachusetts in October 1621. He proclaimed: *"All ye Pilgrims with your wives and little ones, do gather at the meeting house, on the hill ... there to listen to the pastor, and render thanksgiving to the Almighty God for all His blessings."*
- American's first meeting to discuss their future was called the First Continental Congress. A representative from all but one colony gathered in Carpenter's Hall in Philadelphia on September 7, 1774. The meeting started with a three hour long prayer by Episcopal clergy, Dr. Jacob Duche'. Together, they asked for God's guidance.
- The first textbook published in America was originally printed in Boston by Benjamin Harris. It was called *The New England Primer*. It was widely used in the 1600s, 1700s, and well into the 1800s. People were educated using its rhyming alphabet, the Biblical alphabet and the shorter Christian catechism.
- President of the Continental Congress, John Hancock, said as he signed the Declaration of Independence: *"Let us humbly commit our righteous cause to the great Lord of the Universe"*...
- The Declaration of Independence specifically refers to God four times.

- A study of quotations of the Founding Fathers found that 34% were directly from the Bible and 60% were indirectly from the Bible. Our Founding Fathers knew, and were guided by, Scripture.
- George Washington requested the Bible at the time of his inauguration and placed his hand on the Bible as he took the oath of office and is said to have added, "So help me God." All presidents since that time have sworn their oath on an open Bible.
- In 1789, President George Washington proclaimed a day of Thanksgiving saying: "*It is the duty of all nations to acknowledge the Providence of Almighty God, to obey His will and to be grateful for His benefits...*"
- Exactly 50 years after the date of accepting the Declaration of Independence, on July 4, 1826, both John Adams and Thomas Jefferson died.
- In 1865, the last official act by President Abraham Lincoln was the signing into law the adding of "In God We Trust" on all currency.
- The Supreme Court Building has four displays of the Ten Commandments.
- The Declaration of Independence established the nation and the Constitution established the form of government.
- The flag of the United States is handled with care and respect. At the end of the day when taken down by the Armed Forces it is folded and the meaning of the many folds relates to our Christian heritage.
- The Revolutionary War was helped by what was known as the Black Brigade. These were the colonial clergy who inspired the citizens and gave great leadership. Their name came from the pulpit gowns they wore sometimes even on the battlefields.

The Cornerstone of Liberty

Thomas Jefferson once said, *"The Bible is the cornerstone of liberty."*

Acknowledgment of God in Government Buildings
The Washington Monument

Engraved on the capstone is the Latin phrase "Laus Deo," meaning "Praise be to God." Along the walls are Biblical verses such as "Holiness to the Lord" and "Train up a child in the way he should go, and when he is old, he will not depart from it."

The U.S. Capital

The words "In God We Trust" are inscribed in the House of Representatives chamber and over the southern entrance of the U.S. Capital building. Above the Gallery door of the chamber is a relief illustration of Moses surrounded by 22 other law givers.

The Supreme Court

The Ten Commandments are engraved in the two huge doors entering the courtroom and are engraved above the chair of the Chief Justice.

The Highest Glory of the American Revolution

On July 4, 1821, John Quincy Adams said, *"The highest glory of the American Revolution was this:* **it connected,** *in one indissoluble bond,* **the principles of civil government with the principles of Christianity."**

Appendix

Summary of Memory Verses
All references are taken from the New International Version (NIV) Bible.

- Psalms 33:12 - *Blessed is the nation whose God is the LORD, the people he chose for his inheritance.*
- Hosea 4:6 - *My people are destroyed from lack of knowledge.*
- Mark 16:15 - *He said to them, "Go into all the world and preach the good news to all creation."*
- Genesis 2:15 - *The LORD God took the man and put him in the Garden of Eden to work it and take care of it.*
- Leviticus 19:18 - *Do not seek revenge or bear a grudge against one of your people, but love your neighbor as yourself.*
- John 13:34 - *A new command I give you: Love one another. As I have loved you, so you must love one another.*
- Matthew 10:29-31 - *Are not two sparrows sold for a penny? Yet not one of them will fall to the ground apart from the will of your Father. And even the very hairs of your head are all numbered. So don't be afraid; you are worth more than many sparrows.*
- Psalms 127:1 - *….. Unless the LORD builds the house, its builders labor in vain. Unless the LORD watches over the city, the watchmen stand guard in vain.*
- 1 Thessalonians 5:21-22 - *Test everything. Hold on to the good. Avoid every kind of evil.*
- Colossians 2:8 - *See to it that no one takes you captive through hollow and deceptive philosophy, which depends on human tradition and the basic principles of this world rather than on Christ.*
- John 8:31b-32 - *Jesus said, "If you hold to my teaching, you are really my disciples. Then you will know the truth, and the truth will set you free."*
- Psalms 16:1 - *Keep me safe, O God, for in you I take refuge.*
- Leviticus 25:10 - *… and proclaim liberty throughout the land to all its inhabitants.*

Bibliography

- Allison, Skousen, Maxfield, **The Real Benjamin Franklin,** National Center for Constitutional Studies, Washington, D.C., 1982

- Barton, David, **America's Godly Heritage,** WallBuilders, Inc. Aledo, TX 1993

- Barton, David, **The Foundations of American Government,** WallBuilders, Inc., Aledo, TX,1992

- Barton, David, **The Spirit of the American Revolution,** WallBuilders, Inc., Aledo, TX, 2000

- Barton, David, **Setting the Record Straight: American History in Black and White**, Wallbuilders, Inc. Aledo, TX 2003

- Bradford, William, **Of Plymouth Plantation,** 1608-1650, Republished: The Vision Forum, Inc. San Antonio, TX 1998

- Beliles, Dr. Mark, and McDowell, Stephen, **America's Providential History,** Providence Foundation, Charlottesville, Virginia, 1989

- Butler, John, **A Wash in a Sea of Faith, Christianizing the American People,** Harvard University Press, Cambridge, Massachusetts, 1990

- Chalfant, John W., **America: A Call to Greatness**, A Call to Greatness, Inc., Winter Park, Florida 2003, 1996, 1999

- Chapman, Michael J., **Dreamers of a Godless Utopia**, American Heritage Research, 1999, 2002

- DeMar, Gary, **America's Heritage,** Coral Ridge Ministries, Fort Lauderdale, FL, 2002

- Fanella, John Jeffery, **Jonathan Edwards Sinners in the Hands of an Angry God,** P&R Publishing, Phillipsburg, New Jersey, 1996

- Fedderer, William, **America's God and Country, Encyclopedia of Quotations,** Amerisearch, St. Louis, Missouri, 2002

- Iannone, Catherine, **Pocahontas, The True Story of the Powhatan Princess,** Chelsea House Publishers, 1996

- Kennedy, Dr. James, **Foundations for Your Faith**, Fleming Revell, Grand Rapids, MI, 1994

- LaHaye, Tim, **Faith of Our Founding Fathers**, Master Books Incorporated, Green Forest, AR, 1994

- Lillback, Dr. Peter, **Freedom's Holy Light,** The Providence Forum, Bryn Mawr, PA, July 4, 2000

- Lillback, Dr. Peter, **Proclaim Liberty,** Providence Forum, Bryn Mawr, Pa, 2001

- Marshall, Peter and Manuel, David, **From Sea to Shining Sea,** Fleming H. Revell, Grand Rapids, MI, 1986

- Marshall, Peter and Manuel, David, **The Light and the Glory,** Fleming H. Revell, Grand Rapids, MI, 1977

- McDowell, Stephen, **America, A Christian Nation?** Providence Foundation, Charlottesville, Virginia, 2004

- Millard, Catherine, **A Children's Companion Guide to America's History,** Horizon House Publishers, Camp Hill, PA 1960

- McDowell, Stephen and Beliles, Mark, **Liberating the Nations, Biblical Principles of Government, Education, Economic, & Politics,** Providence Foundation, Charlottesville, VA, 1995

- Noebel, David A., **Understanding The Times,** Association of Christian Schools International, Colorado Springs. CO, 1995

- Skousen, W. Cleon, **The Making of America,** National Center for Constitutional Studies, Washington D. C., 1985

Additional Resources

These resources are current as of this printing but are subject to change.

American Heritage Research
Michael J. Chapman
P.O. Box 1291
Minnetonka, MN 55345
http://www.americanheritageresearch.com

Lamplighter Publishing
P.O. Box 777, Waverly, PA 18471
1-888-246-7735
http://www.lamplighterpublishing.com/

Landmarks and Liberty
The Vision Forum Family Catalog
1-800-440-0022, 4719 Blanco Rd.
San Antonio, TX 78212-1015
http://www.visionforum.com/booksandmedia/
- Books, Costumes and Toys

Providence Foundation
434-978-4535
P.O. Box 6759, Charlottesville, VA 22901
www.providencefoundation.com

The Providence Forum
1-866-55-Forum
P.O. Box 446, Bryn Mawr, PA 19010
http://www.providenceforum.org/
- Non-negotiable Teaching Dollar – *A copy of a dollar bill with attached information concerning the writing and symbols.*
- Folding American Flag – *Paper flag with fold lines and meaning of each fold.*
- A life size replica of the Liberty Bell can be on display in your community. Contact the Providence Forum for more information.

Wallbuilders
817-441-6044
P.O. Box 397, Aledo, TX 76009
www.wallbuilders.org
- New England Primer (reprint)
- Posters: Pocahontas
- Numerous books and videos on our Christian Heritage

Meet the Author:
Carol B. Olsen

Since graduating from Iowa State University Carol Olsen has spent more than 40 years in the field of education. She taught high school home economics, coauthored the craft book, *Brass and Beads* and directed and hosted the cable television program, *Mrs. Olsen's Neighborhood*.

As a licensed parent educator Carol developed and provided oversight for a family resource center in the Edina Public Schools system in Edina, Minnesota. Carol saw the public complacency which allowed Christian history of our country to be forgotten or to be eliminated from student history books and all of culture.

As an Elder of Christ Presbyterian Church in Edina, she worked primarily in children's ministry and in 2005 developed a Vacation Bible School curriculum, *Our American Christian Heritage*, for elementary school age children.

For the past 15 years, Carol has taught and lectured both adults and children on our American Christian Heritage and the Christian Worldview.

Carol is married to Neil Olsen, and they have three married children and eight grandchildren, all living in the Minneapolis area.

CPSIA information can be obtained at www.ICGtesting.com
Printed in the USA
BVOW021728081211

277602BV00006BA/4/P